SAVE ME

A CONVERSATION ACROSS THE CITY

A SEARCH PARTY PROJECT
COMPILED BY
BEN FRANCOMBE
JODIE HAWKES
PETE PHILLIPS

ARNOLFINI

University of Chichester

Mayfest

THEATRE BRISTOL

home

Rules and Regs

residence

Compiled by
Ben Francombe, Jodie Hawkes
and Pete Phillips

Designed by
Graham Roy Donaldson

Printed in UK by
MWL Print Group Units 10-13
Pontyfelin Industrial Estate New Inn
Pontypool NP4 0DQ
Tel: 01495 750033
Fax: 01495 751466
www.mwl.co.uk

Published by Arnolfini
16 Narrow Quay
Bristol BS1 4QA, UK
Tel +44 (0)117 917 2300
Fax +44 (0)117 917 2303
www.arnolfini.org.uk

Distributed by
Cornerhouse Publications
70 Oxford Road
Manchester M1 5NH, UK
Tel +44 (0)161 200 1503
Fax +44 (0)161 200 1504
www.cornerhouse.org

ISBN 978-0-9568886-2-4

Book financially assisted by
The University of Chichester
www.chi.ac.uk

Save Me was commissioned
by Mayfest and Theatre Bristol,
with development support by
Home Live Art and Rules and Regs

Editorial Contributions ©
Ben Francombe, Jodie Hawkes
and Pete Phillips 2011

Written contributions ©
Individual authors 2011

Images ©
Individual photographers 2011

CONTENTS

SECTION 1: SEMAPHORE FOR BEGINNERS

Flags fluttering,
tags fluttering,
Jodie and Pete fluttering,
passers-by fluttering,
stewards fluttering,
Bristol fluttering.

Save Me – is all about fluttering: constant movements, little changes, shifts from a distance, people moving on (then returning), traffic perambulating around the city. But the fluttering remains static and retains a sense of purpose: an intriguing impacting scene for a lot of people. We provide an introduction to how, for 11 days in Bristol, semaphore became "some sort of art project".

A   B   C   D   E

N   O   P   Q   R

F   G   H   I   J   K   L   M

S   T   U   V   W   X   Y   Z

We started making a performance called *Save Me* in 2009. It began with an invitation from Rules & Regs to create a new outdoor performance in response to a set of rules devised for White Night Festival in Brighton (UK).

The rules were 1) Get lucky, 2) Illuminate Brighton, and 3) Spend time with an audience. We liked the word 'illuminate', as a method of communication, of clarifying, explaining, making clear, but also in terms of light. Stationed at either end of a busy pedestrian street, using nautical searchlights powered by car batteries, we endeavoured to have a conversation using Morse code. Using lights instead of language, we attempted to test the boundaries of our own intimacy.

Bystanders ran between us, got in the way, sent messages to their own loved ones, complained we were blinding them, tried to decode the messages, told us stories of being in the Navy, flirted with us, drove a wedge between us, encouraged an argument between us and helped us to make amends. Armed with a flask of coffee and a photo of one another, we scrawled our conversation onto the table, painstakingly letter by letter in the dark. We sent messages to each other throughout the night, across a sea of people and like lighthouses facing the darkness we only hoped our messages would get there.

In 2010 we were commissioned by Home Live Art to create a daytime version, so we learnt semaphore. For two days during the Thames Festival, London (UK), with the help of the public, we conversed, Jodie on London Bridge and Pete aboard the HMS Belfast, waving flags along the Thames.

In 2011 Mayfest and Theatre Bristol commissioned a development of our semaphore conversation. We wanted to create a performance that became a part of the landscape that felt strange when it was gone. It was also important for us to find better ways for audiences and bystanders to contribute to our conversation. Inspired by road side memorials and gardens of remembrance, we invited people to write and leave their own messages to loved ones they were apart from on tags tied to our platforms.

Over the course of 11 long days 187 people wrote messages, celebrations, instructions, proposals, regrets and memories. And we were taken aback by the raw emotion of some of these messages, the genuine offers of personal sadness and love, the little glimpses behind the curtains of other people's lives. These messages may never reach their destination, but we wanted to help send them on their way by publishing each and every tag.

Good luck yellow tags.

Jodie & Pete, Search Party.

11 DAYS IN BRISTOL

BEN FRANCOMBE

Saving me; saving _me_ …

For 11 days in May 2011, a drama unfurled across the Bristol skyline. Across the harbour, while boats chugged and buses fumed, passers-by passed by and lingerers lingered and, with constant noises – the drones, the shouts, the snatched laughter, the rumblings of a busy port city – intervening upon spring days, two people spoke. Silently. At a distance. Disrupted from their usual patterns and easy patter by a separating stretch of water: St Augustine's Reach. Yet still they spoke, across water. Using semaphore. This quiet, distant, beautiful, strange conversation had been seen before throughout 2010: in Brighton, in Amiens, in Nottingham, in London: silent talk (using lights at night, then flags by day); a simple, gentle, intervention on to a noisy normality; using language beyond the norm; coded, a special language, almost a private language – as lovers have – to share and celebrate togetherness amongst the throng of a party, say, or a crowded bus: to save themselves from the mundanity of that crowd: 'save me…'; 'save _me_…'

These earlier versions of _Save Me_ already encapsulated much of the empowering dynamic of Search Party's work: a welcoming sense of inclusion; an intervention intended as a shared curiosity with its 'community' rather than a knowing provocation; a performance aesthetic built on that special relationship: a dynamic predicated on love, representing and enveloping Jodie's and Pete's own long-term relationship; an understanding of the urgency of connection and communication in securing and sharing love and the desire to express this in a very public form, without hint of irony.

11 days (then, before and after) …

And so to Bristol. Theatre Bristol and Mayfest commissioned Search Party to present the work for the 11-day duration of Mayfest 2011. Two things immediately became apparent from this commission that would be new to the project: one was the extended time frame, with the implications and pressures of physical endurance and longevity; the other was the place – Bristol – Jodie's and Pete's home for

five years, the centre for much of their creative, social and emotional – not to say, domestic – activity. 'Endurance' and 'home' became buzzwords as we – Pete, Jodie and I (as their dramaturg) – started to fathom out exactly how to frame this work. One thing became clear: _Save Me_ in Bristol for Mayfest 2011 was going to take on significance, distinct in itself.

As this book will attempt to testify, _Save Me_ at Mayfest 2011 has left an important residue of retained responses, memories and concerns that are very much to do with its place but, also, to do with its duration. Of course, it is also to do with its participants – Pete and Jodie and the passers by and the lingerers (whose engaged chatter threw the silent actions of this balletic code into relief). And it was the accentuated silence of _Save Me_, set against the relentless sounds of a vibrant city crowd that started to plot a narrative – or recurring narratives – of separation, and an understanding of a certain kind of separation that emerges, particularly in a city like Bristol.

Bristol has always been an economically vibrant and upbeat city, predicated on trade and commerce, accentuated by its nautical inheritance. Like Hull, Liverpool and Southampton it is a merchant port that does as much (if not more) to define the imperial British inheritance – the gateway to (and from) the 'colonies' – as the Royal-Naval ports of Portsmouth, Plymouth and Chatham. But there is a brutality (or at best a dispassion) to the culture of a merchant port: the steely reality of profit and loss and venture speculation making for a less romantic or nostalgic air: there is none of the rum-rations and farewell-to-you-fair-Spanish-ladies sentimental mythology than emanates from Devonport or Pompey.

To put it bluntly, Bristol is rich: its wealth is manifest (rather than mythologised), remaining in town as an ever evolving, ever consistent display of both individual and municipal satisfaction, so that the stated Eighteenth-Century wealth of Queen's Square, is complimented by the brash re-invention of the docks and harbour as a Twentieth-Century representation of consumption and expendable income.

Conspicuous wealth attracts people: people being a commodity, of course, in Bristol's evolution as a wealthy imperial city. With the slave trade long gone, however, and an ongoing, vigorous, city-wide conversation on the inherited responsibility for that trade, it is easy to assume that, today, a more benign stability is in place in Bristol, making for a more gentle and inclusive municipal dynamic. But Bristol continues to be a place of migration: between 2004 and 2008 a total of 25,600 economic migrants registering for work in the city[1] . These modern-day migrants have as little to do with the easily-identifiable 'leisure-time' wealth of Bristol's dockland as the 'imported' workers of the Seventeenth and Eighteenth Centuries had with the cruising opulence of Queen's Square. Amid the over-easy controversy of immigration – a controversy that easily forgets the uncomfortable propensity of enforced migration – are some pretty hard economic facts. In 2009, the average hourly wage for migrant workers in Bristol was £6.40[2]. Anecdotal reports from this year suggest that plenty of migrant workers are being paid well below the national minimum wage and are working 50-hour weeks and receiving two pay slips – masking the actual number of hours worked[3]. Hardly the grim and haunting brutality of the slave trade, but the challenges of the economic migrant today are very real. The American-based Sociologist, Michael Burawoy, identifies migrant labour as the separation of renewal and maintenance, with a "dual dependence upon employment in one place and an alternate economy and/or state in another" and, thus, "the separation of migrant workers from their families is implied"[4].

Struggling …

The relationship between the migrant worker's long hours, comparatively poor salary and assumed separation from family resonated as a concern for us, in relation to the integral characteristic of separation in *Save Me*. This is very specific to Search Party's characteristic of emotional (loving) connection. Pete and Jodie are working partners, whose domestic (and, therefore, economic) needs are linked to their work. Like all struggling artists (which artist doesn't struggle?), their work is as much defined by their economic and domestic circumstances and increasingly heavy family outlay, as creative inspiration and, again, like all struggling artists, Pete and/or Jodie have to 'migrate' quite a bit in order to pay their way. This leads to a lot of separation. The question of communication across distance in these contexts becomes urgent, made more so – rather than less – by the presumption of modern 'virtual' existence and the easy protocols of digital connection. Leslie Hill, in her exploration of the culture of 'placelessness', suggests that "for many

of us, being physically remote is less of an obstacle to our daily interactions than being without access to email and a cell phone would be"[5]. So, in our so-called shrinking world, we are to suppose, physical place is irrelevant and all Pete needs to do, when, for instance, he travels somewhere to lead workshops or facilitate creative projects, is reach for his mobile and he's connected to Jodie (and if he has to stay overnight, he can Skype, and 'check-in' using Facebook, and log on to Twitter so she knows what he's thinking every twenty seconds…). Digital communication, we are told, has made things easy.

But this easiness is oppressive, because it makes us assume that, in a digital world, communication across distance, sometimes across continents, is, through its immediacy, somehow real. This forces us all to embrace migration as an economic necessity without questioning emotional need. In reality, for Pete and Jodie – for loved ones, generally – when they are apart, the separation from intimacy remains real. For many who are forced into a

separation from loved ones by economic circumstance, the need to find a way to connect becomes critical: the pressures of communication, the need to reach out, to share, to protect, to profess love, to provide strength, becomes so necessary as to render glib technology a falsehood. On one level, therefore, *Save Me* is what Mike Pearson would call an analogue response to a digital world[6]: a slower, step away from presumed, over-easy virtual immediacy. The physical beauty of the act of semaphore – the carefully constructed lettering – reminds us of the traditional tools of reaching across continents. And we don't need to go back to the voyaging pioneers of Bristol's nautical heyday: living memory provides us with resonating images: of letters and telegrams carried by steamboat; five minute phone-calls to New Zealand that cost a month's salary and three weeks to set up; messages sent, by word-of-mouth; shouted greetings over unnatural borders from war-torn places; once-in-a-life-time trips 'home' to places that are no longer home.

LIFE RING

PLEASE REPORT
MISSING LIFE RING
TO THE
HARBOUR MASTER
TEL (0117) 903 1484
STATING LOCATION
NUMBER

THANK YOU

19

A semaphored conversation over the water of St Augustine's Reach allows for a challenge to the placeless easiness of 'virtual' distance.

Semaphore is not easy: it took Pete and Jodie a while to learn and, at first, they were a bit awkward, a bit slow. Reading the transcripts from their 11-day conversation, it becomes clear that they get things wrong and they can't quite achieve a resonating poetry or the spiky soap-opera that we initially hoped would emerge as a result of the recurring feature of the project. But what 11 days gave Jodie and Pete was the chance to get better: they found a way to make this work, to open up, to talk about important things, to share fragments of others' sense of distance and separation, other sets of priorities, and to find new ways to connect and to say things. It is the physical toil connected to the recurring (11-day) presence of *Save Me* that restores the orientation and meaning – the placeness – of the city. Semaphore shows us that short conversations can be poetic and beautiful, and they are poetic and

beautiful because their contained nature makes them painfully resonant – and carefully placed – in a world of over-easy pronouncements.

Fluttering …

While all this was discovered, understood, shared and celebrated, through Mayfest 2011, it was the even shorter pronouncements of separation on the yellow tags, fluttering in a kind of parallel universe throughout the project that motivated this book. When flag semaphore emerged as a method of communicating on the early Nineteenth Century battlefields of Europe, there were, despite the inherent advantages of a lightweight, easily portable system of communication, obvious disadvantages. Aside from its worthlessness at night or in fog, the most obvious problem was of telegraphing your message to all who could see it. Semaphore has no privacy settings: it might be a conversation between two people,

but one that has to be shared. Of course the passers by and the lingerers on Pero's Bridge or at the Fountains could not decipher the semaphore – although many, using the Search Party semaphore crib sheet, certainly tried – but, then again, the black boards, with the emerging conversation written up by the stewards, made deciphering less the point. The point was that many, many people chose to stop, to consider the distance and the silence set against the business of the cityscape, and to reflect upon their own separations. Invited to share these reflections on yellow tags, and to (ritualistically?) tie these tags to the frames of the towers used by both of them, these contributors started to create scenes at each end of St Augustine's Reach that became akin to Scottish clootie wells: organic places of pilgrimage, with fluttering pleas of supplication, emerging as spaces of significance by the accumulation of the most humblest of offerings. Clootie wells have their rags; *Save Me* has its tags, but their shared power is in the overwhelming numbers of people wishing to make an offering, to seek a shared empathy, to contribute to a reflective community.

Like all organic shrines, the fluttering accumulation of yellow-tagged reflections represented a certain need to retain: to enact an almost defiant and halting ritual of awareness and remembrance that flies in the face of an ephemeral or virtual existence. Many of the contributors were from Bristol, many more were not, but all felt happy to allow a personal memory or reflection to become part of the city landscape for a time. And when the time came to call a halt to the act of speaking, the semaphored performance, it became difficult to bring this act of fluttering reflection to an end. The 'residue' that seems so appropriate with so much of Search Party's work is here… At the end of 11 days, the towers are dismantled, the boards stored (or reused for other events), the red clothes are washed and put away, the flags rolled up. But what of the tags? Placed in two linen bags, taken home and… what now? Away from the site and the

public celebration and shared unity of the event, these tags became more resonant in themselves. Jodie and Pete found themselves protective of these little scraps of paper, reading and re-reading, swapping and sharing: laughing, wondering, questioning, analysing… Each one important, irrespective of content or style; each one an act of trust … Something to celebrate, something to share. And so this book emerged as an act of preservation, a way to retain the feelings of strength that came from this shared community: a new meaning to *Save Me*, perhaps? *Preserve* me in physical form and remember that little rituals of strength allow us to keep our loved ones close, even when they are a long, long way away.

[1] See Glossop and Faiza (2009) 'Accession to Recession: A8 migration in Bristol and Hull', Centre for Cities. www.centreforcities.org/assets/files/Accession%20to%20Recession%20.pdf

[2] ibid.

[3] ibid.

[4] Michael Burawoy (1976), "The Function and Reproduction of Migrant Labor: Comparative Material from Southern Africa and the United States", *American Journal of Sociology*, 82(5): pp1050 – 87.

[5] See Leslie Hill and Helen Paris (ed). (2006) *Performance and Place*. Basingstoke: Palgrave Macmillan, p3.

[6] Mike Pearson, Unpublished paper "Who are you looking at? Or: analogue responses to a digital world", presented in a number of conferences/symposia, specifically the Centre for Research in the Arts, Social Sciences and Humanities, Cambridge, 12 March 2009.

SORE ARMS. SORE EYES. SORE FEET.

JODIE HAWKES & PETE PHILLIPS

How do I tell you everything I want to when I have so little time to do it? How do I tell you everything when there are only these few pages? How do I tell you everything when my words fail to say what I mean? Or you fail to understand them? How do I speak of the past six years, when I'm not sure what to leave in and what to leave out? How do I tell you about 11 days? 11 long days. When you weren't there the whole time? When you're not here now? And of course anything I say might be different to what Pete will tell you. Or someone else will tell you, or what I might have told you if you had asked me in May and not in September.

We've long since stepped down from our platforms, the flags
have been packed away and our memories of 11 days on
a bridge/by the fountains are already fading. In the
attempt to reflect on our opposing experiences
of *Save Me* we're going to continue the
discursive nature of the performance by
taking turns. Jodie and I have recently
got into the habit of taking turns,
we've been making work by
sending letters to each
other.

This is our attempt to tell the story of 11 days of semaphore from our perspective(s). Jodie writes in red, Pete writes in yellow:

Firstly, ouch.
She looks so small in the distance and I haven't got binoculars.
Sore arms. Sore eyes. Sore feet.
I'm terrified I'm going to drop one of these flags into the water.
It is an epic task finding a baby sitter for 11 days, we have to make an excel spread sheet of who's picking up and dropping off.
'So where's the other fella…?'
'She's over there by the fountains, she's wearing red'.
The first time I practice on my platform I get vertigo, really not very nice vertigo. I'm worried someone will push me off, or I'll be making an R and misplace my foot. For a few hours we worry there is no way I can do this. We worry that this won't happen.
'Do you know semaphore then…?'
'Yes, I do'.
'Are you making it all up as you go…?'
'Yes, I am.'

I worry someone might push you over. I worry the wind might blow you into the water, and only I know you really aren't that great a swimmer.
'Are you two really together?'
'Yes.'
'Really together, in real life…?'
'Yes'.
The platforms we stand on have to be wheeled along the cobblestones. For a silent performance the set up is excruciatingly noisy.
'Can I leave a message? Will you send it? It's her wedding day/it's our anniversary/he won't get out of bed/I want her to marry me/I don't know where he is/I never got to say goodbye…' 'Yes, leave a message, I will send it for you.'
I feel like Clark Kent quick changing in the toilets of Watershed. When I emerge Chris de Burgh is on the harbourside singing LADY IN RED.
Every morning I say hello to the man selling the Big Issue on the bridge. 'How's it all going?' he says.
'Really well' I say.
Across all this water you make me smile. No one else knows what you just said to me, we share a moment

and I feel closer to you than I ever have.
It's raining. Hard. More like hail stones. I'm still here waving my flags. Everyone else has run for cover. I'm in the middle of a message. I keep going. But the message doesn't get through – Jodie has been wrestling with a PVC poncho. She missed the whole thing.
At the fountains a group of primary school children are trying to decipher your message, there's a drunk woman trying to get on my platform and signal for me, there's so much wind, everything is blowing away, there's a lady who has just found out she has cancer and needs me to send a message, there's a man from the sight seeing bus who wants to know what's going on, there's someone who's been with Pete who tells me I'm getting it all wrong, there's a guy asking if I've got a boyfriend, and a family who don't speak English leaving a message to someone, somewhere out there.
I want to tell you about this story that someone over here told me, it's quite long, and there are quite a few details that I can't edit out. It's going to take a while, but I think it's important.

2 3

Really it's only a few sentences but when I have to spell out each letter with a wave of these flags it starts to drag. But stick with it. Stick with me. It's worth it. It's going somewhere. My face is already sore from all this squinting.

I arrive on the bridge with my flags, ready to set up and tied to the railings is one yellow tag. Its plastic bag still has last night's raindrops speckled in its creases. It's been there all night. Someone took it away with them, sat down, thought about what to write and when they returned I had gone – so they tied their tag to the bridge, like a roadside memorial. I read it. I leave it there. Karenzza, that's a really beautiful name.

And the boats go under the bridge and they wave. I wave back. And the boats go under the bridge and they smile. I smile back. And the boats keep sailing in and out, and for 11 days we keep exchanging waves and smiles. I swing my flags and knock someone really, really hard on the head.

And the tags keep coming. People write them, read them, take them away and bring them back.

My favourite type of audience member (if I'm allowed a favourite) is the older man who hangs out by the side for what seems like a good hour, who has a look on his face of pure reminiscence. He doesn't come over. He occasionally gives me a knowing nod and smile, as if to say 'I'm in on it'. There are lots of this man.

The first time we meet the saxophone player it's clear we're on his patch, his turf. He's not angry, it's clear he's done this before and the unpredictability of busking doesn't faze him. But still, I get the impression he'd prefer to be where I am and that I wasn't waving my flags on his bridge... A week later and I'm still here on this bridge and we meet the saxophone player again. And now it's ok, he takes up another pitch and looks over with a sense of acceptance – and after seven long days I start to belong here. It's raining, no, hailing. I'm stuck in a poncho. I mean really stuck. My head is in the arm hole.

I hand the message you've just sent to Abbie (the Steward) to be written up on the chalkboard, and I'm composing my response and someone says, 'she's not finished, she's waving her flags, she's trying to say something.' And you are. And despite the 500m of water and boats and trees and swans and seagulls between us, I feel like I still can't get a word in edgeways. I ignore you and send my own, really long message back. You spend ages in between messages fiddling with your flags, drinking water, reading the tags, thinking of what to say, speaking to people passing by. I'm so sick of waiting for you. I curse you under my breath.

I can't think of anything to say. And I know you're waiting. And I know you're getting angry, you're thinking 'come on Pete, what's taking so long, say something, say anything, what are you doing?' But the chalk pens are running out, I'm tired, the wind is too strong, I'm squinting, and I don't have anything to say. When it is windy the flags feel twice as heavy. I struggle to move them. I feel the pain later. When the wind has gone, waving the flags feels less important, less skilled, less emotive. I wish for the wind and all its arm ache.

Three men walk past. They're drunk at 11:30am. 'Go on, jump!' they say.

I see a man searching through the tags. I've seen him before, a day or two ago in the pouring rain. Now he's scanning the PREVIOUSLY ON SAVE ME board. So I ask him if he would like to write a message and he tells me that he already has and that I've already sent some of it. He shows me a rain splattered tag about someone called Karenzza and I say 'Yes what a beautiful name'. And then he tells me about what happened. And I'm a little lost for words. I say 'I'm really sorry to hear that' and I feel silly for saying it. And I say can I tell Pete you're here? And he says 'yes'. And he comes back again and again and again searching for his messages, searching for his tag, searching for his part in this story.

And now your B's are starting to droop, your L's are looking laboured, I can't distinguish your P's from your Q's and I have never been able to get my head round those last few letters of the alphabet which don't get used so often.

You send something terribly romantic and I have a brief moment where I see my boyfriend all the way over there, on a bridge, sending me a message with flags and it is really rather beautiful.

11 days feels like a really long time. It feels like it's never going to end. I just want it to end. I'm tired of all this flag waving, tired of all the tears and regret, I'm tired of everyone who did it in scouts or guides or cadets. I'm tired of all the yellow tags and I'm tired of standing here in this red jumper.

We arrive on day 11 to find Heart FM have a stand in the exact place I should be semaphoring. There's no way to move it. It's the Bristol 10K race and the harbourside is transformed into a silver foil wearing, tannoy speaking, water drinking place. There's a different sort of effort and duration here today. We have to wait a few hours before we can begin and I really don't want this to end.

The stewards are starting to flag, they stop wearing their t-shirts and handing out their programmes. We're all starting to feel it.

Everyone around me is crying. I'm not sure if it's all this effort, or being so tired, or that I'll never be here doing this again, or that I've been listening and hearing all these stories of loss and heartache. But everything goes in slow motion, blurry and as I spell out 'Enough now. I'm tired'. Goodbye arm ache. Goodbye sore eyes' the tears roll down my cheeks.

I want this to be over.

After the 11 days are over, we wonder what we should do with all these messages. We cut the yellow tags off the platforms and feel very guilty. We keep them in bags in the kitchen. Other people's messages for people out there tucked away in our kitchen. We spend a few hours reading them all. We wonder what we should do. How we could get the messages out there. We have meetings with Ben around the kitchen table, over lunch and decide we should put them here in a book. We hope that's ok.

SECTION 2:
11 DAYS IN MAY

So, Jodie and Pete are isolated and separated, for 11 days, yet they talk … This section is all about that.

We see them isolated, on their towers; we see them exposed to the elements and exposed to the curiosity of people; we see the stretch of water and the sense of distance, as well as perspective (Jodie's side or Pete's); we see each day in turn. And, most of all we read what they said (well, what they semaphored). We see how it was documented and how the process of recording opens up the idea that what we say is not always what we hear (or, in this case, see) and, in order to understand one form of communication (semaphore) through another (the written word), we have to interpret, guess, impose punctuation, adapt …

The conversations have been lovingly typed up by Jodie in a clear act of translation. But what to translate? What she 'sent' to Pete or what Pete 'received'? What she received from Pete or what he sent? We can't quite decide, so what has been typed is what each of them received (taken from the board from the receiver's end), but we have felt a need to annotate: to explain, to clarify, to punctuate, to justify. We have also started to comment, to explore, to check, to question, to analyse, to mess about. These conversations, between two people, have become very public sharing's: short, controlled, encoded; … but shared.

THINGS YOU MIGHT NEED FOR AN 11 DAY SEMAPHORE CONVERSATION:

- 4 handmade semaphore flags
- 2 good red pens
- Someone you miss
- 2 plastic ponchos (in case of rain/hail/sleet/snow)
- 2 strong arms (each)
- 6 red reporters notepads from the Post Office with string for your necks and paper clips for the wind
- Binoculars (in case your eyes get sore)
- Some distance
- 11 days… 11 long days
- An embrace
- Some fireworks
- A marching band
- A good working knowledge of semaphore
- Something red to wear so you can be seen in the distance
- A framed photograph of you (for them)
- A framed photograph of them (for you)
- Cable ties. Glue. Tape

- Chalk pens (Yellow, Red, White)
- A nice hand to copy it all out for you
- Stage weights or sand bags
- 2 platforms
- 4 chalk boards
- Black paint
- Tears
- Sun tan lotion (in case the weather takes a turn for the better)
- Lots and lots of handmade yellow tags (for other people to join in)

- Water to keep you going
- Your own unique signal for 'HOLD ON, I'M LOST, START AGAIN, SLOW DOWN, PLEASE LETS START OVER'
- A busking licence
- The Harbourmaster's permission
- Child care
- Patience
- A bit more patience
- Arm ache
- Sore eyes
- Hope

Save me

- New idea
- Site visit — practical
          — show Ben

Oasis

31

SAVE ME...

...RIDAY 6TH MAY	DAY 3 : SATURDAY 7TH MAY	DAY 4 : SUNDAY 8TH MAY	DAY 5 : MONDAY 9TH MAY
...DNESDAY 11TH MAY	DAY 8 : THURSDAY 12TH MAY	DAY 9 : FRIDAY 13TH MAY	DAY 10 : SATURDAY 14TH MAY

3 2

DAY 1:

THURSDAY 5TH MAY 2011

Weather
Clear, slight breeze.
Highs of 16°.

JODIE: I HOPE YOU CAN SEE ME OK IT'S GONNA BE 11 LONG DAYS UNTIL I SEE YOU UP CLOSE AGAIN

PETE: YES I CAN SEE YOU. RIGHT NOW 11 DAYS FEELS LIKE A REALLY LONG TIME

JODIE: YOU KNOW WHAT THEY SAY DISTANCE MAKES THE HEART GROW FONDER

PETE: I THOUGHT IT WAS ABSENCE? HOW DOES YOUR HEART FEEL NOW?

JODIE: FEELS STRANGE I WONDER IF THIS IS SOMETHING LIKE PERO FELT

PETE: WELL I'M ON HIS BRIDGE AND FROM HERE I CAN STILL MAKE YOU OUT IF I SQUINT

JODIE: YES I GUESS HE NEVER GOT TO SEE HIS LOVED ONES AGAIN

PETE: I HEARD A STORY ABOUT A SET OF TWINS WHO WERE REUNITED AFTER SEVENTY YEARS APART

JODIE: WHAT HAPPENED WHEN THEY SAW EACH OTHER?

PETE: I'M NOT SURE BUT AFTER SEVENTY YEARS I'D EXPECT A FEW TEARS

JODIE: OR FIREWORKS

PETE: OR A MARCHING BAND

JODIE: EVERYTHING GOES SLOW MOTION

PETE: LIKE THE TORTOISE WHO GOT LOST. IT WAS THE FIRST TIME BERT HAD BEEN AWAY FROM DAISY SINCE NINETEEN FIFTY FIVE

JODIE: YES OR THE MEN WHO COME BACK FROM SEA FROM WAR FROM THE MOON

PETE: MAYBE IN ELEVEN DAYS WHEN WE ARE REUNITED WE WILL BE REMEMBERED AS WELL

JODIE: I HOPE YOU STILL REMEMBER ME... SAY SOMETHING

PETE: RIGHT NOW I CAN STILL PICTURE YOUR FACE. I HOPE THE PICTURE STAYS CLEAR WHILE WE ARE APART

JODIE: LET'S HOPE

Pete's board

Day 1: Thursday 5th May 2011

Jodie: I hope you can see me ok. It's ~~gonna~~ *going to* be ~~11~~ *eleven* long days until I see you up close ~~again~~.

Pete: Yes I can see you. Right now ~~eleven~~ *eleven* days feels like a really long time. — *264 hours*

Jodie: You know what they say distance makes the heart grow fonder.

Pete: I thought it was absence. ~~&~~ How does your heart feel now?

Jodie: Feels strange. I wonder if this is something like Pero felt?

Pete: Well I'm ~~here~~ on his bridge and from here I can still make you out if I squint.

St Augustine's Parade (Photo St of sore eyes)

Jodie: Yes I guess he never got to see his loved ones again.

Pete: I heard a story about a set of twins who were reunited after seventy years apart.

Jodie: What happened when they saw each other?

Pete: I'm not sure but after seventy years I'd expect a few tears.

Jodie: Or fireworks.

Pete: Or a marching band.

approx 25,550 days together.

Jodie: Everything goes slow motion.

Pete: Like the tortoise who got lost. It was the first time Bert had been away from Daisy since nineteen fifty five.

Jodie: Yes or the men who came back from sea, from war, from the moon.

Pete: Maybe in eleven days when we are reunited we will be remembered as well.

Somewhere between 225,622 miles and 252,088 miles. (rocket) - 3 days, 3 hours, 49 minutes.

Jodie: I hope you still remember me.

Pete's semaphore is so slow today

~~Pete:~~ *Jodie* Say something.

Pete: Right now I can still ~~picture~~ *pic* ~~x~~ your face. I hope ~~to~~ *the* picture stays clear while we are apart.

Jodie: Let's hope.

35

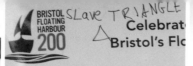

END-OF-DAY

We asked Jennie Dick, one of our stewards, to document
the team's thoughts and feelings at the end of each day

- "Easier to see Jodie as she has trees behind her, whereas Pete has red industrial-ness behind him".

- "A woman purposefully choosing to be late for her 1 o'clock meeting as she wanted to take photos and write a tag".

- "Being told off by the Harbour Duty Officer as we were blocking his bridge".

- "A woman opening up and telling me about her first long distance relationship, it was her first love, he was in the Navy, it was twenty years ago. Strange how willing people are to openly talk to a stranger".

- "The view of Jodie and Pete signalling across the water as a little kid paddled in the fountain and office workers solemnly ate their sandwiches and looked on".

- "The 25th wedding anniversary tag that was written on the bridge podium".

- "The wind. It was really windy".

- "When asked by a scribe if punctuation is needed on the boards Pete replied "Write what I write. Punctuation is assumed as in any spoken communication".

DAY 2:

FRIDAY 6TH MAY 2011

Weather
Clear, slight breeze.
Highs of 15°.

FRIDAY 6TH MAY

JODIE: HELLO PETE OVER HERE WE ARE MISSING YOU. OVER HERE PEOPLE HAVE BEEN LEAVING MESSAGES FOR THEIR LOVED ONES

PETE: WHAT HAVE THEY BEEN SAYING

JODIE: MESSAGES TO BETTER PLACES, TO KENYA, TO NURSERY, TO LIVERPOOL TO WORK, TO BACK HOME IN BED

PETE: WHO ARE THE MESSAGES FOR

JODIE: TO MUM, TO ANNA, TO THE LOVE OF MY LIFE, TO KATIE

PETE: YESTERDAY STEPHEN AND JANET LEFT A MESSAGE OFER HERE

JODIE: WHO ARE THEY?

PETE: THEY WERE CELEBRATING THEIR SILVER WEDDING ANIVERSARY AND THEY HAVE NEVER BEEN APART

JODIE: NEVER?

PETE: NEVER. THEY ALWAYS TRY TO SAY WHAT THEY FEEL INCASE THEY ARE EVER APART

JODIE: SOMETIMES ITS HARD TO SAY WHAT YOU REALLY MEAN

PETE: ESPECIALLY WHEN YOU ARE SO FAR AWAY

JODIE: SOMEONE OVER HERE WANTS SOMEONE CALLED BEAR TO MARRY THEM

PETE: DO YOU WANT TO MARRY HIM

JODIE: NOT ME, SOMEONE ELSE

PETE: ARE THEY WAITIN FOR AN ANSWER

JODIE: YES, THE WAITING IS THE WORST BIT BUT THERES HOPE OVER HERE

PETE: I READ A STORY ABOUT A SOLDIER WHO PUT A MESSAGE IN A BOTTLE AND HOPED CT WOULD GET TO HIS LOVER ACK HOME

JODIE: DID IT EVER FIND HER?

PETE: IT ARRIVED TWENTY YEARS AFTER SHE HAD DIED BUT IT WAS DELIVERED TO HER GRANDDAUGHTER

JODIE: BUT IT MADE IT ACCROSS ALL THAT WATER

PETE: YES A FISHERMAN CALLED STEVE FOUND IT NINETY EIGH YEARS LATER

JODIE: I HOPE SOME OF OUR MESSAGES HERE MAKE IT TO THEIR LOVED ONE

these conversations are ~~our responses~~ for the messages we each recieved. In red on top is what we sent (plus punctuation).

Day 2: Friday 6th May 2011

Jodie: Hello Pete, over here we are missing you. Over here people have been leaving messages for their loved ones.

Pete: What have they been saying?

4,305 miles (boeing 707) - 10.1 hrs

Jodie: Messages to better places, to Kenya, to nursery, to Liverpool, to Work, *to* back home in bed.

to mine
1.9 miles
(walking) 37 mins

Pete: Who are the messages for?

181 miles
(car) - 3 hours 12 mins

Jodie: To ~~Luv~~ *MUM*, to Anna, to the love of my life, to Katie.

Pete: Yesterday Stephen and Janet left a message over here

Jodie: Who are they?

Pete: They were celebrating their silver wedding aniversary and they have never been apart.

25th year anniversary
celebrated with silver gifts

Jodie: Never?

Pete: Never, they always try to say what they feel incase they are ever apart.

Jodie: Sometimes its hard to say what you really mean.

~~I miss you~~
~~I love you~~
~~I don't feel the same~~

Pete: Especially when you are so far away.

Jodie: Someone over here wants someone called Bear to marry ~~me~~ *them*.

Pete: Do you want to marry him?

Jodie: Not me, someone else.

Pete: Are they waiting for an answer?

Jodie: Yes the waiting is the worst bit but there's hope over here.

Pete: I read a story about a soldier who put a message in a bottle and hoped it would get to his lover back home.

Jodie: Did it ever find her? *?*

Pete: It arrived twenty years after she had died, but it was delivered to her grandaughter.

Approx 7,300 days later

Approx 35,770 days after

Jodie: But it made it across all that water.

Pete: Yes a fisherman called Steve found it ninety eight years later.

Jodie: I hope some of our messages here make it to their loved ones.

42

END-OF-DAY

- "Old man genuinely concerned : 'What are you doing? Summoning German submarines?'".

- "I know semaphore I learnt it at scouts/school/brownies/girl guides all those years ago" (lots of reminiscent OAPs).

- "French couple: 'Do. You. Speak. French?', Jennie: 'Not much', French man: 'Woah. You speak too fast'. Managed to have a whole conversation in slow disjointed French and English".

- "More buggies than business people today".

- "Jodie is very observant on what is happening around her and can respond to the public as well as concentrating on flags and writing".

- " The crowd were clambering to leave messages".

- "Today was a sad day, very reminiscent and emotive".

- "Abby (Pete's scribe) started to explain the piece in fluent French to some young French people. A universal performance!".

- "A college boy compared the piece to a site specific piece he did where he was a bird, a pigeon, who acted like a tourist. Can't see the similarities myself".

DAY 3:

SATURDAY 7TH MAY 2011

Weather
Fairly breezy.
15° in the AM.

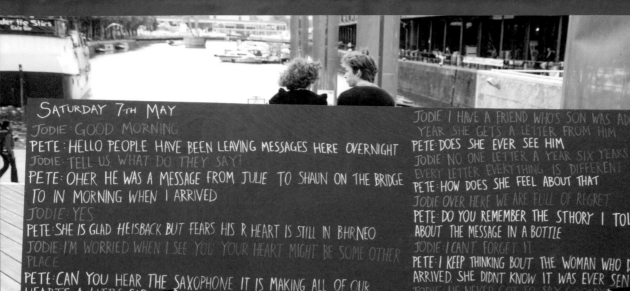

Jodie's board

Day 3: Saturday 7th May 2011

Jodie: Good morning.

Pete: Hello, people have been leaving messages ~~here~~ overnight.

Jodie: Tell us what do they say?

Pete: ~~ohor he~~ There was a message from Julie to Shaun on the bridge ~~to in~~ this morning when I arrived.

Jodie: Yes

Pete: She is glad ~~heisback~~ he is back but fears his heart is still in Borneo

7280 miles (fly) 15 hours 30 mins

Jodie: Im worried when i see ~~you~~ your heart might be some other place.

Pete: Can you hear the saxophone? It is making all of our hearts a little sad.

we're on his patch

Jodie: Just the sounds of ~~the city~~ Bristol we say come home, ~~hime~~ we say good luck, we say don't go.

Pete: The saxophone plays and we say we can't afford a ring, we say don't feel guilty, we say dont be alone.

Jodie: We say I miss you, I miss you, I miss you.

Pete: I miss you to and there are still eight days untill we are reunited, I hope nothing has changed?

192 hours

Jodie: like what?

Jodie: I have a friend who's son ~~is~~ was adopted, Every year she gets a letter from him.

Pete: Does she ever see him?

Jodie: No, One letter a year, six years, six letters, every letter every ~~tt~~ thing is different.

Pete: How does she feel about that?

2190 days approx

Jodie: Over here we are full of regret.

Pete: Do you remember the ~~st~~ story I told you yesterday about the message in a bottle?

Jodie: I can't forget it.

Pete: I keep thinking about the woman who died before it arrived. She didnt know it was ever sent.

Jodie: He never got to say goodbye.

4253 miles (flying) - 6843.08 kilometers 10 hours?

Jodie: I have a message to Lynett in ~~Trinidad~~ Trinandad who never ever said goodbye.

Pete: The soldier said goodbye, but his lover never got to hear it.

The bridge was empty except for one rain soaked tag tied to the railings. It must have been there all night.

47

END-OF-DAY

- "Quieter than Friday – strange for the centre of Bristol".

- "When people are around a larger group will form – safety in numbers".

- "Girl Guide leader excited by the performance – took a few leaflets, wants to teach her guides".

- "Mother of two boys wanting to know if we know anywhere where the boys could learn semaphore because they were so interested".

- "More people appeared surprised it was a performance today – odd, we had a sign and everything".

- "Man to wife on bridge: 'Semaphore…..a forgotten skill'".

- "There was an extremely enthusiastic old lady talking about semaphore in the Girl Guides".

- "When asked if they wanted to write a tag a passer-by said 'I don't have anything interesting to write' – the idea that because it may be read by others assume it has to be interesting to those around".

- "The saxophonist adding a sombre tone".

- "Jennie: 'Would you like to fill in a tag?', Lady 1: 'I am not in the right place to write this', Lady 2: 'Completely understandable'. Must have touched a nerve".

- "A conversation with the saxophonist asking what we were doing led to the statement 'Oh – you are real time too'".

- "Liked the little yellow tag, covered in rain, waiting for him on the bridge one morning".

DAY 4:

SUNDAY 8TH MAY 2011

Weather
Excessively windy
with moments
of rain and hail.
Highs of 17°.

PETE: I'M STILL HERE. LAST NIGHT I WAS THINKING ABOUT A STORY THAT SOMEONE OVER HERE WAS TELLING ME.

JODIE: WHAT DID THEY SAY?

PETE: THEY WERE TELLING ME ABOUT THEIR GRANDMOTHER WHO LIVED IN NEW ZEALAND

JODIE: YES.

PETE: THIS WAS BEFORE YOU COULD FLY THERE. THE BOAT TOOK MONTHS.

JODIE: I SEE.

PETE: HER SISTER WAS GETTING MARRIED IN THE UK.

JODIE: WHAT HAPPENED?

PETE: SHE HAD TO BOOK A THREE MINUTE PHONE CALL THREE WEEKS IN ADVANCE.

JODIE: AND SHE GET TO SPEAK TO HER?

PETE: I THINK SO BUT IT MADE ME WONDER WHAT WOULD YOU SAY?

JODIE: HOW DO YOU TRAVERSE THOUSANDS OF MILES HALF THE GLOBE IN THREE MINUTES? WHAT SO MANY THINGS TO SAY.

PETE: I DON'T KNOW WHAT I WOULD HAVE SAID. SOMETIMES I DON'T KNOW WHAT TO SAY TO YOU.

JODIE: OVER HERE WE HAVE SO MANY THINGS TO SAY AND NOT ENOUGH TIME.

PETE: THESE FLAGS ARE TOO SLOW. WHAT DO YOU WANT TO SAY?

JODIE: OVER HERE WE SAY, MUM IN LIVERPOOL I FEAR I WILL NEVER SAY I LOVE YOU ENOUGH TIMES BEFORE YOU ARE GONE.

PETE: OVER HERE WE SAY TELL HER THERE IS STILL TIME.

JODIE: OVER HERE WE SAY FATHER IN NEW ZEALAND I WANT TO PATCH THINGS UP IT'S BEEN TOO LONG I MISS YOU.

PETE: AND WE SAY PATCH THINGS UP. MAKE AMEDS.

JODIE: WE SAY LOVELY MAN TOO NEAR BUT TO FAR CAN WE BE TOGETHER IN ANOTHER LIFETIME

PETE: OVER HERE WE SAY WHY DON'T YOU COME BACK.

JODIE: OVER HERE WE ARE WET WE ARE TIRED OUR ARMS ACHE

PETE: OVER HERE WE ARE SHIVERING MY EYES ARE SORE BUT THE SAXOPHONE STILL PLAYS.

JODIE: WE HEAR IT. PLEASE DON'T GIVE UP ON ME.

PETE: I WON'T. I WILL BE HERE ON THIS BRIDGE WAITING FOR YOU.

Pete: I'm still here, last night I was thinking about a story that someone over here was telling me.

Jodie: What did they say?

Pete: They were telling me about their grandmother who lived in New Zealand.

11,395 miles
(plane) - 23 hours 23 mins

Jodie: Yes?

Pete: This was before you could fly, the boat took months. *there,*

Jodie: I see.

Pete: Her sister was getting married in the UK.

Jodie: What happened?
Jodie: What happened? — *180 seconds*

Pete: She had to book a three minute phone call, three weeks in advance.

Jodie: And she get to speak to her? *did*

Pete: I think so but it made me wonder what would you say? *t*

Jodie: How do you traverse ~~thousands of miles~~ ~~half the globe~~ in three minutes? *half the globe, thousands of miles,* ~~what~~ so many things to say.

Pete: I dont know what I would have said, sometimes I dont know what to say to you.

Jodie: Over here we have so many things to say and not enough time.

Pete: These flags are too slow, what do you want to say?

Jodie: Over here we say Mum in Liverpool, I fear I will never say I love you enough times before you are gone.

Pete: ~~Over~~ here we say tell her there is still time. *Over*

Jodie: Over here we say father in New Zealand I want to patch things up it's been ~~too~~ long I miss you. *to my* *so*

Pete: And we say patch things up, Make amends. *p*

Jodie: We say lovely man too near but too far can we be together in another lifetime?

Pete: ~~Over~~ here we say ~~hydryck~~ *Over* *why don't you come back.*

Jodie: Over here we are wet, we are tired our arms ache.

Pete: Over here we are shivering, my eyes are sore, but the saxophone still plays. *we are still on his patch*

Jodie: We hear it, please dont give up on me.

Pete: I wont, I will be here on this bridge waiting for you.

END-OF-DAY

- "The idea of physical and emotional distance".

- "Excessively windy day (very painful wind) signs blew over due to lack of preparation – not enough cable ties".

- "A huge moment of panic – Charlotte dropped the weight on her foot, Jodie got down off of the podium".

- "A real sense of togetherness – people beginning to understand the convention – people returning, wanting to know the story".

- "The determination of Jodie and Pete throughout the downpour".

- "Hail stone message. Misinterpreted. Natural elements effecting communication".

- "Great to see returning people".

- "I want to send a message to someone I had a meal with last night, he was embarrassing and I am angry about it".

- "Woman returning to write her tag today because 'it all got a bit much yesterday' – still didn't leave one today – tears in her eyes – it's for a 'special man'".

FOUR DEPARTURES IN SEVEN AND A HALF YEARS, IN CHRONOLOGICAL ORDER

SAINI MANNINEN

Departure no. 1

Event: My grandmother dies.

Distance: Pretty insurmountable.

Communication: Minimal and one-sided. Mainly based on my memories of her final months. I imagine her sitting in her rocking chair at Christmas opening her presents. I imagine her sticking her tongue out whenever someone takes a photo of her. I imagine her walking next to me in the winter. I imagine her lying in her hospital bed with burning hands and ice cold feet.

Lost: A grandmother.

Gained: Too early to say.

Departure no. 2

Event: I move to a different country leaving behind my family, friends and my homeland.

Distance: 1160.5 miles.

Communication: First email, then increasingly Skype and Facebook, postcards and parcels in the post, text messages. Biannual trips back. I bought my best friend a notebook in which we could write letters to each other and keep sending it back and forth. She mostly forgets to send it back and by the time she does she has already written two letters in it and I have heard most of her news through Facebook. Still, it's always nice to see her handwriting.

Lost: The birthdays of the people whose birthdays don't coincide with my biannual trips. The daily sorrows and joys of friends. Seeing my goddaughter grow, which she does rapidly. She sent me a postcard from her trip to Stockholm with no text but only a picture of her which she had drawn. I knitted her a purple chick called Pauline for Easter.

Gained: A new country. Free chocolate and sweets that my mother sends.

Departure no. 3

Event: My sister moves to the other side of the world.

Distance: 10175.4 miles.

Communication: Skype, emails and parcels in the post. Three face to face encounters in four and a half years. Our Skype conversations start with a hello, then a pause, a grin and a slight bafflement as to how we should proceed. What do you say? I often say, so what have you been up to? It's easier that way; when I ask what she's been up to she can tell me about her day because it's her night time whereas I would have got up only a couple of hours earlier. In the pauses during our conversations we stare at each other and then pull faces. (To compensate for hugs, I imagine.) When we say bye bye we wave in an exaggerated manner.

Lost: Being able to touch her pregnant belly.

Gained: A salad bowl, a teapot and three soft toys that didn't fit in her luggage.

Departure no. 4

Event: I move to a new city after four years in one place leaving behind good friends and professional support networks.

Distance: 98.5 miles.

Communication: So far, email and postcards. I changed my desktop background to a picture of a friend. She's standing with her back to the camera, holding an owl on her outstretched arm. She's looking at the owl and laughing. I imagine that's one of her most exciting memories.

Lost: Support networks and shared lunch breaks.

Gained: A sense that these departures will keep happening. In the space between here and there, I compose lists of important things that I need to tell them about when I see them next. In the space between here and there, my grandmother keeps poking her tongue out at every camera and in that space I imagine every conversation in the instant technology realm to be free of any awkward pauses.

And I imagine my goddaughter growing and growing and growing until she towers above everyone and everything like a skyscraper. And every departure has a trace of all the previous departures and every time I imagine the distances will get a little shorter.

PREVIOUSLY

DAY 1: THURSDAY 5TH MAY

JODIE: I HOPE YOU CAN SEE ME OK IT'S
GOING TO BE 11 LONG DAYS UNTIL I SEE YOU
UP CLOSE AGAIN
PETE: YES I CAN SEE YOU. RIGHT NOW
11 DAYS FEELS LIKE A REALLY LONG TIME
YOU KNOW WHAT THEY SAY DISTANCE
MAKES THE HEART GROW FONDER
PETE: I THOUGHT IT WAS ABSENCE? HOW DOES
YOUR HEART FEEL NOW?
JODIE: FEELS STRANGE. I WONDER IF THIS IS
SOMETHING LIKE PETE FELT
PETE: WELL I'M ON HIS BRIDGE AND FROM
HERE I CAN STILL MAKE YOU OUT IF I SQUINT
JODIE: YES I GUESS. WE NEVER GOT TO SEE
HIS LOVE COMES AGAIN

PETE: I HEARD A STORY ABOU
WERE REUNITED AFTER SEV
JODIE: WHAT HAPPENED WHE
PETE: I'M NOT SURE BUT AFT
EXPECT A FEW TEARS
JODIE: OR FIREWORKS
PETE: OR A MARCHING BAND
JODIE: EVERYTHING GOES SLOW
PETE: LIKE THE TORTOISE WHO
FIRST TIME BERT HAD BEEN AWA
NINETEEN FIFTY FIVE
JODIE: YES OR THE MEN WHO CAM
FROM WAR. FROM THE MOON
PETE: MAYBE IN ELEVEN DAYS
WE WILL BE REMEMBERED
JODIE: I HOPE YOU STILL REMEMBER
PETE: RIGHT NOW I CAN STILL F
THE PICTURE STAYS CLEAR WHIL
JODIE: LET'S HOPE

60

DAY 5:

MONDAY 9TH MAY 2011

Weather
Humid.
Highs of 17°.

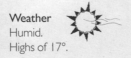

MONDAY 5TH MAY

PETE: HELLO JODIE HELLO MONDAY

JODIE: HELLO PETE OVER THE PAST FOUR DAYS I'VE MET LOTS OF PEOPLE HERE AT THE FOUNTAINS

PETE: YES

JODIE: THROUGH SUN, RAIN AND BRACING WIND EVERYONE HAS SOMETHING TO SAY WE ALL HAVE PEOPLE WE ARE APART FROM

PETE: ARE YOU OK?

JODIE: OVER HERE THE WIND IS TOO STRONG OVER HERE. HERE WE HAVE SO MERE_UEST

PETE: WHAT ARE THE PEOPLE BY THE FOUNTAINS HOPING FOR?

JODIE: OVER HERE HERE WE ARE SAYING FOUR MONTH OLD KAYLA IN HOSPITAL GET WELL SOON MY DARLING

PETE: OVER HERE WE SAY GET WELL SOON

JODIE: AND WE SAY KARENZA IN CORNWALL, IN HEAVEN I MISS YOU EVERYDAY AND WISH YOU WEREN'T TAKEN FROM ME AFTER I FOUND YOU AGAIN

PETE: THE WIND IS TAKING YOU AWAY FROM ME. BUT THE WIND IN YOUR FACE IS THE SAME WIND ON MY BACK

JODIE: IT'S WHISPERING STORIES OF LOVED ONES OF PERO OF YOU

PETE: OVER HERE WE SAY I CARRIED YOU FOR SEVEN WEEKS I WISH YOU WERE HERE WITH ME

JODIE: AND AT THE FOUNTAINS WE SHOUT WE WILL NEVER FORGET

PETE: AND WE SAY WE ARE BRAVER FOR CONCEIVING YOU

JODIE: AND WE SAY WE WISH YOU SAFE JOURNEY

PETE: OVER HERE SOMEONE HAS LEFT A MESSAGE FOR THEIR BOYFRIEND IN OXFORD

JODIE: I'M LOSING YOU OVER HERE OUR EYES ARE SORE

PETE: STAY WITH ME

JODIE: NOT SURE IF I CAN

PETE: PLEASE STAY WITH ME. WE HAVE SO MUCH TO SAY TO YOU

Pete's board

Day 5: Monday 9ᵗʰ May 2011

96 hours

Pete: Hello Jodie, Hello monday.

Jodie: Hello Pete. Over the past four days I've met lots of people here ~~at~~ *by* the fountains.

Pete: Yes?

AND HAIL

Jodie: Through sun, rain, and bracing wind everyone has something to say, we all have people we are apart from.

Pete: Are you ok? (LONG PAUSE)

I have to stop flag waving for the first time due to the strong winds.

Jodie: Over here the wind is too strong, over here ~~here~~ we have ~~so more uest~~ *some requests*

Pete: What are the people by the fountains hoping for?

Jodie: Over here ~~here~~ we are saying four month old Kayla in hospital get well soon ~~my~~ darling.

Pete: Over here we say get well soon.

Jodie: And we say Karenza in Cornwall, in heaven, I miss you everyday and wish you weren't taken from me after I found you again.

Karenzza
Karenzza ~~~~
~~~~ who's
~~~~
boyfriend came back to stand next to me to look for his rag nearly every~day

Pete: The wind is taking you away from me, but the wind in your face is the same wind on my back.

Jodie: It's whispering stories of loved ones, of Pero, of you.

Pete: Over here we say i carried you for seven weeks, I wish you were here with me,

Jodie: And at the fountains we shout we will never forget.

Pete: And we say we are braver for conceiving you.

Jodie: And we say we wish you safe journey.

Pete: Over here someone has left a message for their boyfriend ~~no ford~~ *oxford.*

Jodie: I'm losing you, over here our eyes are sore.

Pete: Stay with me.

Jodie: Not sure if i can.

Pete: Please stay with me. We have so much ~~left to say~~ *to say to you.*

85.4 miles (car) - 1 hour 33 min

END-OF-DAY

- "OAP male: 'can you pass the message, on tsunami due at 3pm'".

- "Man: 'What are you doing?', Jennie: 'A performance called *Save Me*, this is Search Party, here we have Jodie and there on the bridge ... etc etc', Man: 'Why?', Jennie: 'It's part of Mayfest ... etc etc', Man: 'Not being rude but why?', Jennie: 'It is exploring the idea of communication, intimacy across distance, 'slow motion' communication, long distance relationships', Man: 'Why? What does it actually do?', Jennie: 'It is causing a reaction – people feel something from this. Thinking of lost loved ones, people across the miles or even their pets sitting at home. Getting a chance to say what you haven't before', Man: (still a little vacant) 'Oh. Ok'".

- "When trying to decipher codes Abby realised that Pete and Jodie were going too fast, never thought I'd say semaphore was too fast".

- "The name and the story of Karenzza is beautiful".

- "Two teenage boys walking past 'what day are we on?' – having a catch up".

- "The most muscley OAP ever – used to be a merchant sailor – knows his semaphore".

DAY 6:

TUESDAY 10TH MAY 2011

Weather
Bright, scattered
showers.
Highs of 18°.

PETE: GOOD MORNING JODIE WE'RE ALMOST HALF WAY. I CAN ALMOST SEE THE LIGHT AT THE END OF THE TUNNEL

JODIE: I'VE BEEN THINKING ABOUT THE LAST TIME I SAW YOU FIVE DAYS AGO

PETE: WHAT DO YOU REMEMBER ABOUT ME?

JODIE: ALL THE GOOD STUFF. OVER HERE BY THE FOUNTAINS WE WON'T LET GO

PETE: OVER HERE ON THE BRIDGE WE LIVE TOO FAR FROM OUR MOTHERS

PETE: WE WISH WE WERE CLOSE ENOUGH TO POP IN FOR A CUP OF TEA

JODIE: AND WE STILL SAY COME HERE, DON'T GO, WE NEED YOU

PETE: SOMEONE ON THE BRIDGE TOLD ME A STORY ABOUT THE NATIONAL EXPRESS

JODIE: WHAT DID THEY SAY?

PETE: HIS GIRLFRIEND WAS GOING AWAY FOR A WHILE SO HE TOOK HER TO THE BUS STATION TO SAY GOODBYE.

JODIE: YES, AND?

PETE: AND WHEN THE MOMENT CAME TO SAY GOODBYE HE COULDN'T

JODIE: SO WHAT DID HE DO?

PETE: HE GOT ON THE BUS WITHOUT A TICKET, WITHOUT ANY LUGGAGE, HE DROPPED EVERYTHING TO BE WITH HER

JODIE: AND OVER HERE YOUR STORIES ARE MAKING PEOPLE BY THE FOUNTAINS SMILE

PETE: EARLIER TODAY YOU SAID 'YOU WON'T LET GO' WHICH REMINDED ME OF THAT STORY

JODIE: WHY WON'T YOU LET ME SPEAK?

JODIE: LET ME FINISH THINGS ARE HAPPENING HERE TO WE HAVE THINGS TO SAY

PETE: TELL ME

JODIE: WE SAY MY BROTHER AT WORK I THINK YOU ARE MAD AT ME BECAUSE I DIDN'T SAY THANK YOU

PETE: AND WE SAY FORGIVE ME BROTHER WE ARE GRATEFUL

JODIE: AND WE SAY HANNAH IN OXFORDSHIRE HAVE YOU FED THE CAT

PETE: WE SAY FEED THE CAT HANNAH FEED HIM FEED HIM

JODIE: AND WE SAY SKYE OUR DOG IN KENNELS IN SCOTLAND WE MISS OUR WALKS BUT BRISTOL IS LOVELY

PETE: AND WE SAY WE LOOK FORWARD TO SEEING YOU AGAIN

JODIE: AND I SAY I'M SICK OF WAITING

PETE: HOLD ON. HOLD ON. WE'LL SEE EACH OTHER AGAIN SOON. HOLD ON.

Pete's board

BoLD — Day 6: Tuesday 10th May 2011

Pete: Good morning Jodie, we are almost halfway I can almost see the light at the end of the tunnel.

Jodie: ive been thinking *ALOT* about the last time I saw you five days ago.

Pete: What do you remember about me?

The first time I met you on that bus, my 21st birthday party, that couting crows concert, your cooking, the creases by your eyes, your gold tooth, Wakefield, Exeter, dulwich,

Jodie: all the good stuff. Over here by the fountains we wont let go.

Pete: Over here *O* in the bridge we like too *K* far from our mothers.

Pete: We wish we were close enough to pop in for a cup of tea.

Jodie: and we still say come here, dont go, we need you.

Pete: Someone on the bridge told me a story about the national express.

Jodie: what did they say?

Pete: *His* was girlfriend was going away for awhile so he *took* tok her to the bus station *(in Wakefield)* to say goodbye.

It wasn't raining and you weren't soaking wet and Interest didn't sorry for you out there all wet.

Jodie: yes and?

Pete: And when the moment came *to* ta say goodbye he couldnt.

Jodie: so what did he do?

Pete: He got on the bus without a ticket, without any luggage, he dropped everything to be with her,

Jodie: and over here your stories are making people by the fountains smile.

Pete: Earlier on today you said *(you* we wont let go' which reminded me *of that* other story.

Jodie: why wont you let me speak WHY WONT YOU LET ME SPEAK?

LET ME FINISH!
Jodie: let me finish Things are happening here to we have things to say.

Pete: Tell me?

Jodie: we say my brother at work I think *your* you are mad at me because I didnt say thank you?

Pete: And we say forgive me brother we are grateful.

Jodie: And we say Hannah in Oxfordshire have you fed the cat?

Pete: We say feed the cat hannah feed him. Feed him.

Jodie: and we say Skye our dog in kennels in Scotland, we miss

*On foot ... 610 miles
4 days 1 hour*

our walks but bristol is lovely.

Pete: And we say we look forward to seeing you again.

Jodie: and i say im sick of waiting.

Pete: Hold on. Hold on. Well see each other again soon. Hold on.

69

END-OF-DAY

- "Woman: 'Do you mind if I have another yellow tag – I wrote one yesterday but I kept waking up in the night thinking of more appropriate and better things to say'".

- "A man reads every 'previously on' photo and laughs out loud".

- "How un anything specific the piece is; no set age, sex, race, nationality".

- "Why is there the lie of not seeing each other?".

- "Makaton sign language – similarities".

- "Japanese tourist – absolutely fascinated by the concept: 'WOW, WOW'".

- "Great location – encouraging people to view theatre who wouldn't usually get a chance".

- "Disabled and special needs group staying and interacting and a foreign exchange group also engaged. Impressed by the versatility of the piece".

PETE: HE GOT
LUGGAGE, HE D

JODIE: AND O
BY THE FOUN

PETE: EAR
WHICH RE

JODIE: W

JODIE: LE

WE HAVE

73

DAY 7:

WEDNESDAY 11TH MAY 2011

Weather
Cloudy and cool.
Highs of 19°.

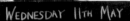

Jodie's board

WEDNESDAY 11TH MAY

JODIE: HELLO PETE HELLO WEDNESDAY OVER HERE BY THE FOUNTAINS IT IS STARTING TO FEEL LIKE HOME

PETE: WHAT DO YOU MEAN HOW DO ES IT FEEL LIKE HME

JODIE: OVER HERE WE HAVE NEW FRIENDS, NEW HOPES, OVER HERE YOU ARE FADING INTO THE DISTANCE

PETE: OVER HERE ON THE BRIDGE IT FEELS LIKE THISGS HAVE CHANGED

JODIE: AND WE SAY WE ARE TOO BUSY WE SAY WE ARE FORGETTING

JODIE: AND AT THE FOUNTAINS I'M WITH MY MOTHER IN DEVON I'M WITH MY GRANDFATHER IN HEAVEN

PETE: WE SAY WE MISS YOU. GRANDFATHER WE MISS YOU

JODIE: AND WE SAY JOANNA IN SOUTH AMERICA I'M SORRY I WISH I KNEW HOW YOU WERE

PETE: COME HOME SAFE POANNA OR WRITE OR CALL WE ARE WORRIED

JODIE: BUT SOME OF US HERE AT THE FOUNTAINS SAY YOU CAN'T MAKE US WE DON'T WANT TO COME BACK

PETE: AND ON THE BRIDG WE SHOUT WE DON'T WANT YOU BACK

JODIE: AND WE ARE LOSING INTEREST WE ARE FORGETTING TO WATCH INCASE YOU ARE WAITING

PETE: AND I SAY I AM CLOSING MY EYES SO I CAN FORGET YOU AND THOSE FOUNTAINS

JODIE: AND I WHISPER LET ME GO LET ME GO LET ME GO

PETE: I DONT KNOW WHAT TO SAY TO YOU DO YOU REMEMBER STEPHEN AND PANET

JODIE: YES MAYBE THEIR FIREWORKS HAVE GONE TOO

PETE: MAYBE THEIRFIREWORKS WENT LONG AGO BUT THEY DIDNT GIVE UP

JODIE: THE PEOPLE AT THE FOUNTAINS SAY PATCH THINGS UP MAKE AMENDS OUR HEARTS ARE STILL BEATING

PETE: KEEP BEATING PODHIES HEART KEEP GOING JODIES ARMS AND JODIES FLAGS KEEP WAVING

JODIE: ILL TRY EVEN HARDER

PETE: ON THE BRIDGE WE SAY DAD THINGS DONT NEED TO BESODIFFERNT

JODIE: WE SAY JIM SCULL THANKYOU FOR HELPING ME THROUGH THE TOUGH TIMES

PETE: THANKYOU JIM THANKYOU FOR UNDERSTANDING

JODIE: AND THANKYOU ON THE BRIDGE ILL SEE YOU TOMORROW ILL BE HERE WAITING

PETE: I CAN STILL PICTURE YOUR FACE TOMORROW THEN

76

Jodie: hello pete,hello wednesday.over here by the fountains it is starting to feel like home.

Pete: what do you mean,how does it feel like home?

Jodie: over here we have new friends,new hopes,over here we are fading into the distance.

you

Pete: over here on the bridge it feels like things have changed.

Jodie: and we say,we are too busy,we say,we are forgetting.

A few hours?
Under 100miles approx

Jodie: and at the fountains i'm with my mother in devon,with my grandfather in heaven.

Pete: we say we miss you grandfather,we miss you.

Jodie: and we say joanna in south america,i'm sorry,i wish i knew how you were?

8645 miles approx?

Pete: come home safe joanna.or write,or call.we are worried.

Jodie: but some of us here at the fountains say you cant make us,we don't want to come back.

Pete: and on the bridge we shout we don't want you back!

Jodie: and we are losing interest,we are forgetting to watch in case you are waiting.

Pete: and i say i am closing my eyes so i can forget you,and those fountains.

you

Jodie: and i whisper let me go,let me go,let me go.

Pete: I don't know what to say to you.do you remember Stephen and Janet?

Jodie: yes maybe their fireworks have gone too?

Pete: maybe their fireworks went long ago,but they didnt give up.

their fireworks

Jodie: the people at the fountains say patch things up,make amends,our hearts are still beating.

Pete: keep beating jodies heart,keep going jodies arms and jodies flags,keep waving.

Jodie: ill try even harder.

Pete: on the bridge we say dad things don't need to be so differnt.

Jodie: we say jim scull thank you for helping me through all the tough times.

Pete: thank you jim.Thankyou for understanding.

Jodie: and thank you on the bridge,ill see you tomorrow,ill be here waiting.

Pete: I can still picture your face,tomorrow then.

PREViOUSLY ON SAVE ME...

| DAY 1: THURSDAY 5TH MAY | DAY 2: FRIDAY 6TH MAY | DAY 3: SATURDAY 7TH MAY | DAY 4: SUNDAY 8TH MAY | DAY 5: MONDAY |

DAY 7: WEDNESDAY 11TH MAY   DAY 8: THURSDAY 12TH MAY   DAY 9: FRIDAY 13TH MAY   DAY 10: SATURDAY

END-OF-DAY

- "Man in his 50s, when informed it was a performance and in fact not in the navy the response was– 'She's in the navy, I'm gonna join the navy next week in 'port-mouth'".

- "Suddenly had a nervous moment, sudden stage fright and didn't want to talk to people".

- "Lady with small child 'this is making me weep (tears streaming down her face) this is beautiful'. Her yellow tag said: To: Mark. Where: On the other side of death. What: I hope you are still dancing. I still miss you".

- "Feels like we have been doing this forever".

- "Can't see the end".

- "Long, tiring day, seemed to go really slowly".

"WHAT'S ALL THIS THEN ... SOME KIND OF 'ART' PROJECT?"

We're a few days in, and an inquisitive scattering of passers-by are gathering at the foot of Jodie's pedestal. It's a foreboding sky, and the wind whips at the flags like a bird in flight. A man to the left of me, is standing very still, he squints into the distance trying to get a better view of where she is reaching out to. To Pete. "what's all this then, ?" he asks. "some kind of art project?". Well, er, yes I begin the spiel, 'they are sending messages to each other...' I refer to the programme, point dutifully at the semaphore diagrams. He makes me feel faintly ridiculous. "do they know each other" he continues, frown deepening. "Well yes, they do. Very well. They live together. They have a child". "Well, why don't they just speak to each other then?...got something to say why doesn't she just go over there and say it to him". I'm stumped. But he stays put, and takes the leaflet from my hand. And when I return later on, he is still there. Telling someone next to him all about it. Explaining about the messages. Smiling.

Kate Yedigaroff (Mayfest)

DAY 8:

THURSDAY 12TH MAY 2011

Weather
Cloudy with spells
of sunshine.
Highs of 15°.

JODIE: HELLO PETE THIS TIME LAST WEEK WE STOOD ON THESE
PLATFORMS FOR THE VERY FIRST TIME
PETE: I REMEMBER
JODIE: THE SUN WAS SHINING ON MY FACE AND HERE I AM AND SO MUCH HAS
HAPPENED
PETE: ON THE BRIDGE WE'VE SEEN MARRIAGE PROPOSALS AND
WEDDING ANNIVERSARIES
JODIE: WHAT ELSE?
PETE: WE'VE HAD HEARTS IN BORNEO AND MOTHERS IN NEWCASTLE
JODIE: AND WE'VE LEFT SPACE IN A BED FOR YOU
JODIE: AND I'M STILL WAITING FOR YOU EYES FIXED
PETE: WE'RE WAITING ON THE BRIDGE TOO WAITING TO BE REUNITED
JODIE: AND OVER HERE WE SAY MY AUNT IN A HOME REMEMBER
THE GOOD TIMES
PETE: NEVER FORGET THE GOOD TIMES
JODIE: ALL THIS LOOKING BACK ITS MAKING ME LONELY
PETE: DO YOU KNOW THE STORY ABOUT MICHAEL COLLINS?
JODIE: NO WHO IS HE?
PETE: HE WAS ONE OF THE APOLLO ELEVEN ASTRONAUTS
JODIE: YES
PETE: HE WAS THE COMMAND MODULE PILOT FOR THE FIRST MOON
LANDING
JODIE: I SEE DID HE COME BACK?

PETE: YES BUT WE WERE TALKING ABOUT BEING LONELY. HE
STAYED IN THE SPACE SHIP WHILE THE OTHER TWO WALKED ON THE
MOON
JODIE: ALL ON HIS OWN?
PETE: WHEN HE PASSED BEHIND THE DARK SIDE OF THE MOON
HE COULDN'T SEE THE EARTH
JODIE: COMPLETE DARKNESS
PETE: HE EXPERIENCED AN ALONENESS UNKNOWN TO MAN
PETE: OUT OF SIGHT OUT OF RADIO CONTACT COMPLETELY
ALONE
JODIE: WE ARE STILL LONELY FOR KARENZA MIKE HAS COME
BACK HE STILL MISSES HER
PETE: WE SAY MY DEAR NESSOOTJE MAKE A DECISION
A GOOD ONE
JODIE: I'M FINDING THIS HARD I'M SORRY I'M FINDING THIS HARD
I WANT TO GIVE UP SEVEN DAYS AND I CAN'T UNDERSTAND YOU
PETE: DON'T GIVE UP DON'T STOP WAVING YOUR FLAGS
JODIE: I HAVE SO MANY THINGS TO SAY AND I DON'T KNOW HOW TO
SAY THEM
PETE: TOMORROW IS A NEW DAY THERE IS STILL TIME

Pete's board

Day 8: Thursday 12ᵗʰ May 2011

Jodie: Hello Pete, this time last week we stood on these platforms for the ~~very~~ first time.

Pete: I remember.

Jodie: The sun was shining on my face and here I am and so much has happened.

Pete: On the bridge ~~we k sen~~ _we've seen_ marriage proposals and wedding aniversaries.

Jodie: What else?

Pete: We've had hearts in (Borneo) and ᵐbrothers ⁱⁿ(Newcastle).

13hrs 42mins approx
6846miles approx
(air)

Jodie: And we've left ᵃspace in a bed for you.

246 miles
5hrs 3mins
(car)

Jodie: And I'm still₍ₐ₎ _struck here_ waiting for you eyes fixed.

Pete: We're waiting on the bridge too,ø waiting to be̲reunited.

Jodie: And over here we say my Aunt in a home remember the good times.

Pete: Never forget the good times.

Jodie: All this looking back it's making me lonely.

Pete: Do you know the story about Michael Collins?

Jodie: No who is he?

Pete: He was one of the Apollo eleven astronauts.

Jodie: Yes?

Pete: He was the command module pilot for the first moon landing.

20ᵗʰ July
1969

Jodie: I see did he come back?

Pete: Yes, but we were talking about being lonely. He stayed in the spaceship while the other two ~~we lke~~ _walked_ on the moon.

space here

Jodie: All on his own.

Pete: When he passed behind the darkside of the moon he couldn't see the the earth.

Jodie: Complete darkness.

Pete: He experienced an aloneness unknown to man.

Out of sight,   Previously?

Pete: ~~Wet hfsig t~~ out of radio contact, ~~or~~ completely alone.

Jodie: We are still lonely for Karenza̅. Mike has come back he still misses her.

Pete: We ~~bary~~ _Say_ my dear Nessoot ̶w̶e make a decision, a good one.

Jodie: I'm₍,₎ finding this hard, ~~I'm sorry Im finding this hard~~ _sorry I'm_ I want to give up. ~~seven days and~~ _seven days and_ I cant understand you.

Pete: Don't give up, don't stop waving your flags.

Jodie: I have so many things to say and I don't know how to say them.

Pete: Tomorrow is a̲new day, there is still time.

END-OF-DAY

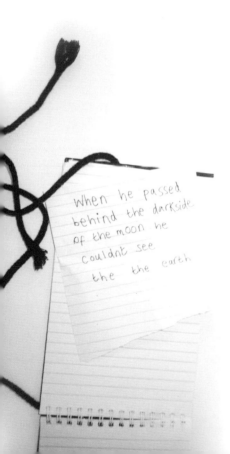

When he passed
behind the darkside
of the moon he
couldn't see
the the earth

- "Lots of ex-navy and merchant navy. People enjoy the connection. Lots of reminiscing".

- "School children wanting to learn".

- "*Save Me* – available and accessible for all ages".

- "The willingness of strangers to talk to you. Loneliness?".

- "Lady learnt semaphore as a girl – communicates with her family across the bay in Cornwall".

- "The enthusiasm of a group of school children – some had learnt semaphore as Scouts and Brownies".

- "Mike (Karenzza story) returning each day".

- "Two homeless people with Alzheimer's relating to the piece. An Indian family giving a full story about who they were away from. Again – willingness to talk".

DAY 9:

FRIDAY 13TH MAY 2011

Weather
Cloudy, slight wind.
Highs of 13°.

FRIDAY 13TH MAY

PETE: GOOD MORNING JODIE HELLO FRIDAY THERE IS NOT LONG LEFT NOW CAN YOU HEAR THE MARCHING BAND
JODIE: YES WE HAVE THE CHAMPAGNE ON ICE
PETE: SAVE A GLASS FOR ME WELL BE TOGETHER AGAIN SO ON A MAN HERE IS WAITING TO BE REUNITED WITH PEFFERY
JODIE: WE HAVE MESSAGES TOO FOR BARRY FOR MORGAN FOR MIRIAM FOR MIKE FOR BEHLA
PETE: OHAT DO THEY SAY WHAT SHOULD WE SAY TO BARRY AND THE OTHERS
JODIE: WE SAY MY NEIGHBOUR SOPHIE THANKYOU FOR COMING OUT WHEN YOU HEARD ME THANKYOU FOR CALLING NINE-NINE NINE THANKYOU FOR SAVING MY LIFE
PETE: THANKYOU SOPHIE THE HERO AND WESAY TO OUR RAMILY IN BLACKPOOL WE WISH YOU WERE HERE WE WISH YOU COULD SEE THIS
JODIE: AND WE SAY TO MUM AND DAD IN BAHRAIN THANKYOU FOR ALL YOU'VE DONE AND ALL THAT YOU DO FOR ME
PETE: AND WE SAY TO BILL IN NEW YORK I DONT KNOW WHETHER TO COLF AND JOIN YOU
JODIE: AND TO ARIEL IN KENTUCKY THE CLOCK IS TICKING
PETE: TO THE OLD US BEFORE THE TWO BABIES DONT GIVE UP THE HOPE LETS NOT FORGET WHO WE WERE
JODIE: TO MARK ON THE OTHER SIDE OF LIFE ARE YOU STILL DANCING
PETE: MY EYES ARE SORE I BLINK AND I MISS YOUR WORDS BLINK BLINK BLINK

JODIE: TRY HARDER BE STRONGER FOR JOHN AND MANDY AND MATT AND MO
PETE: AND FOR MY FAMILY ACROSS THE SEA HUNDREDS OF MILES APART I DONT KNOW WHEN ILL SEE YOU AGAIN
JODIE: I HOPE NOT TOO LONG REMEMBER THE CLOCK IS TICKING AND IF YOU SEE ELLA IN BRISTOL ASK HER IF SHE IS OK WE ARE WORRIED PLEASE CALL LINDA AND SIMON
PETE: WE HAVENT SEEN ELLA ON THE BRIDGE BUT WELL KEEP LOOKING WELL KEEP ASKING COME HOME ELLA
JODIE: AND I SAY COME HOME PETE LET THIS BE OVER AT THE FOUNTAINS MY ARMS ARE ACHING
PETE: AND ON THE BRIDGE WE ARE RUNNING OUT OF SPEAM
JODIE: BUT THINK OF THE MARCHING BAND THE CHAMPAGNE THE LONG EMBRACE
PETE: UNTIL TOMORROW THEN

Day 9: Friday 13th May 2011

Pete: Good morning Jodie. Hello Friday. there is not long left now. can you hear the marching band ?

Jodie: Yes we have the champagne on ice .

Pete: Save a glass for me. We'll be together again soon. A man here is waiting to be reunited with Jeffery.

Jodie: We have messages too for Barry, for Morgan, for Miriam, for Mike, for Bella .

Pete: What do they say? what should we say to Barry and the others ?

Jodie: We say my neighbour Sophie, thank you for coming out when you heard me, thank you for calling nine nine nine, thank you for saving my life.

Pete: Thankyou Sophie the hero, and we say to our family in (Blackpool), we wish you were here, we wish you could see this .

208 miles
3hrs 32mins
(car)

Jodie: And we say to Mum and Dad in (Bahrain), thank you for all you've done and all that you do for me .

3371 miles
6hrs
44mins
(air)

Pete: And we say to Bill in (New York) I don't know whether to come and join you .

3268 miles
6hrs 32mins
(air)

Jodie: And to Ariel in (Kentucky) the clock is ticking.

3942 miles
7hrs 53mins
(air)

Pete: To the old us before the two babies. don't give up the hope, lets not forget who we were .

Jodie: To Mark on the other side of life, are you still dancing ?

Pete: My eyes are sore. I blink and I miss your words. Blink blink blink .

Jodie: Try harder, be stronger, for John and Mandy and for Matt and Mo .

Pete: And for my family across the sea, hundreds of miles apart, I don't know when ill see you again .

Jodie: I hope not too long. Remember the clock is ticking and if you see Ella in Bristol ask her if she isok, we are worried, please call Linda and Simon .

Pete: We haven't seen Ella on the bridge but we'll keep looking, we'll keep asking. Come home Ella .

Jodie: And I say come home Pete let this be over. At the fountains my arms are aching .

Pete: And on the bridge we are running out of steam .

Jodie: But think of the marching band, the champagne, the long embrace .

Pete: Until tomorrow then .

93

END-OF-DAY

- "Man with Morse code – telling the story of planes landing in Australia – the lights went so cars headlights were used to light the runway".

- "The temporary yet permanent trust the public put in us – to talk to and to write such personal tags on the podiums".

- "The idea of shooting the messenger – if the semaphore messenger is shot then how do they communicate? Big flags make them an easy target".

- "The lady with the 999 tag. To: Sophie my old neighbour. Where: In the house next to my old one. What: Thank you for mopping up my blood, thank you for calling 999. You helped to save my life. When she handed me the tag I'd thought what a grumpy woman, so rude. Then I read the tag after she left".

- "A lady had leukaemia, had just found out and had to tell her daughter. Got very emotional about the piece".

DAY 10:

SATURDAY 14TH MAY 2011

Weather
Clear.
Highs of 15°.

PETE: GOOD MORNING JODIE. HERE WE ARE AGAIN. YOU BY THOSE FOUNTAINS AND ME ON THIS BRIDGE

JODIE: HELLO PETE HELLO SATURDAY HELLO SUNSHINE HELLO THAT BRIDGE

PETE: TOMORROW IS THE LAST DAY FOR US. WE'LL BE TOGETHER AGAIN BUT FOR THE PEOPLE WHO HAVE LEFT MESSAGES THIS ISN'T OVER

JODIE: AT THE FOUNTAINS SOME PEOPLE NEVER COME BACK I HOPE YOU COME BACK TO ME

PETE: DO YOU REMEMBER WE TALKED ABOUT MICHAEL COLLINS THE ASTRONAUT?

JODIE: YES WE REMEMBER. WE REMEMBER EVERYONE WE HAVE SPOKEN OF

PETE: A MAN ON THE BRIDGE REMEMBERED WATCHING IT ON TV

JODIE: WHAT WAS HE SAYING?

PETE: HE SAID COLLINS BIGGEST FEAR WAS COMING BACK TO EARTH ALONE. WITHOUT THE OTHER TWO

JODIE: BUT AT THE FOUNTAINS WE SAY YOU ARE SAFE NOW NO MORE SUFFERING YOU ARE FREE

PETE: HE WAS AFRAID OF LEAVING A HERO AND COMING BACK AS SOMETHING ELSE

JODIE: OVER HERE WE HAVE ALL LEFT SOMEBODY OVER HERE WE SAY BE BRAVE WE'LL SEE YOU AGAIN SOME DAY

PETE: WE SAY BE BRAVE ON YOUR WEDDING DAY - HUG THE WORLD

JODIE: AND WE SAY FORGET THE RING I LOVE YOU MADLY TRULY DEEPLY

PETE: OVER HERE WE SAY TO E BETWEEN MOSCOW AND BRISTOL. ITS A BEAUTIFUL DAY ON THE BRIDGE

JODIE: AND WE SAY TO OUR LOVED ONES ON THE OTHER SIDE KEEP COMING TO SEE US WE MISS YOU

PETE: OVER HERE WE SAY TO MY SISTER STOOD NEXT TO ME I'M SORRY I DON'T SEE YOU ENOUGH

JODIE: AND TO MY SISTER JO IN YORKSHIRE I MISS THE LITTLE GIRLS WE USED TO BE BUT I'M SO PROUD OF THE PERSON YOU'VE BECOME

PETE: OVER HERE WE MISS OUR FAMILY BACK IN AFRICA I WILL JOIN YOU SOON

JODIE: AND OVER HERE J. WE STILL MISS YOU

PETE: I MISS YOU TOO. CAN YOU HEAR THE SAXOPHONE. HE IS MUCH MORE UPBEAT TODAY. FULL OF HOPE

JODIE: A LITTLE O HEAR THE MARCHING BAND THE FIREWORKS

PETE: I'LL SEE YOU TOMORROW. I'LL BE WAVING MY FLAGS

JODIE: AND I'LL BE WAITING EYES FIXED

Pete's board

Pete: Good morning Jodie. Here we are again, you by ~~tose~~ those fountains and me on the bridge.

Jodie: Hello Pete, hello Saturday, hello sunshine, hello that bridge.

Pete: ~~The orrow~~ Tomorrow is the last day for us. We'll be together again, but for the people who have left the ~~g~~ messages this isn't over.

Jodie: At the fountains some people never come back, I hope you come back to me.

Pete: Do you remember we talked about Michael Collins the astronaut?

Jodie: Yes we remember, we remember everyone we ~~have~~ spoken of.

Pete: A man on the bridge remembered watching it on TV.

Jodie: What was he saying?

Pete: He said Collins biggest fear was coming back to earth alone, without the other two.

Jodie: But at the fountains ~~we say~~ we say you are safe now, no more suffering, you are free.

Pete: He was afrid of leaving a hero and coming a back ~~assolething~~ as something else.

Jodie: Over here we have all left somebody, over here we say be brave, we'll see you again some day.

Pete: We say be brave on your wedding day-hug the world.

Jodie: And we say forget the ring, I love you madly, truly, deeply.

1656 miles
3 hrs 19 mins
(air)

Pete: Over here we say to Ebet ~~we are~~ between Moscow and Bristol, Its a beautiful day ~~here~~ on the bridge.

Jodie: And we say to our loved ones on the other side, keep coming to see us, we miss you.

Pete: Over here we say to my sister stood next to me I'm sorry I dont see you enough.

223.4 miles
3 hrs 58 mins
(car)

Jodie: And we say to my sister Jo in Yorkshire, I miss the little girls we used to be together, Im so proud of the person you've become. but

Pete: Over here we miss our family in Africa, I will amazing join back you soon.

Jodie: And over here we still miss you.

8 hrs 36 mins approx
4300 miles
(air)

Pete: I miss you two. Can you hear the saxophone? he is much more upbeat today. full of hope.

Jodie: A little L we hear the marching band, the fireworks.

Pete: Ill see you tomorrow, Ill be waving my flags.

Jodie: And ill be waiting, eyes fixed.

END-OF-DAY

- "Returning man 'technology man', tweeting about *Save Me* and Search Party every day. Says this is the best Mayfest event. All our conversations have ended with the uses of technology – even though it is about the lack of it".

- "The boat day – capturing video footage of the semaphore from the boat".

- "The reoccurring issue of loneliness of people. A desire to talk off their problems".

- "A difficult day. Returning people didn't need to know what the piece was about".

- "People writing tags even when finished and packed up".

- "A man told a story of his great uncle who had a stroke so started tapping Morse code on his wrist. No one else knew it. Sadly a useless form of communication if another doesn't know it".

Fwd: My attempt at writing something for your book!

Jodie Hawkes [jodie@searchpartyperformance.org.uk]

From: Holly
Date: 19 September 2011 23:47:31 GMT+01:00
To: Jodie Hawkes <jodie@searchpartyperformance.org.uk>
Subject: Re: My attempt at writing something for your book!

Hey Jodie!

I just sat down at the weekend with the request you had posted, and then started writing and this is what came out! I really wanted to get involved with this, especially because the subject matter def strikes a chord with me because of me making the move to usa from uk and all the emotions that it has whipped up! I actually really enjoyed writing this and found it very cathartic, it just flowed out of me quite easily and seemed to complete itself which rarely happens to me! So thank you for setting this homework, and thank you for your lovely words :-)

We definitly should skype soon. Mornings on a sat or sun are good for me so around 1pm onwards english time. Let me know when a good date and time is :-) xxx

Sent from my Samsung Intercept™

A Sea of Separation

Separation is not something that can be quantified; it comes in infinite degrees.

A decision to physically relocate, may seem as if it is opening the chasm of separation. The very land, home, people that have tied you to a place, are being cast off. A decision like that is hard to make, and upon making it you may find yourself drifting in that in-between, separation dividing you from everyone; from those you are planning on leaving behind, because of the distance you are about to stretch between you and from those you are moving towards, because you have not yet arrived. In this place you could let loneliness wash over you, or you could realize the great freedom in your choice. You have not allowed the fear of separation to constrain you, your hopes and dreams have bigger plans, they will not be defeated. Emerging from your decision, is the taking of that first step, on that great journey, and suddenly you are not looking back, at what you are leaving or losing, but looking forward at what you are gaining. Separation over distance, is only one kind of being apart, and there are many ways to diminish the effect of that particular separation. Almost every single thing in life can be a "separation"; time, space, distance, difference, perspective, culture, language; each person decides to what degree they are separated in the world.

Separation can seem huge, and looming, but if you retain perspective, and choose to view it not as a constraint and uncontrollable force but instead as a challenge, that with your strength, can be overcome, you will greatly reduce its size.

Do not allow the sea of separation to engulf you, but rise above its waves, and enjoy the bumpy ride.

DAY 11:

SUNDAY 15TH MAY 2011

Weather
Grey and cool.
Highs of 14°.

Jodie's board

SUNDAY 15th MAY

PETE: HERE WE ARE
JODIE: FOR A WHILE THERE I THOUGHT WED NEVER MAKE IT
PETE: WE MADE IT AND IN TWO HOURS WELLS TOT WAVING THESE FLAGS
JODIE: YES BUT FOR THE PEOPLE AT THE FOUNTAINS IT WONT BE OVER
PETE: TOMORROW THERE WILL BE A SPACE ON THIS BRIDGE WHERE I HAVE BEEN BUT THERE ARE SO MANY MESSAGES HERE
JODIE: AND AT THE FOUNTAINS WE SHOUT GOODBYE PERO GOODBYE THAT BRIDGE GOODBYE ILL NEVER FORGET YOU
PETE: AND WN THE BRIDGE WE SAY GOODBYE ELVEN LONG DAYS GOODBYE FOUNTAINS GOODBYE THE WIND AT MY BACK
JODIE: GOODBYE BABY I CARRIED FOR SEVEN WEEKS GOODBYE GRANDAD IN HEAVEN GOODBYE KARENZZA WELL MISS YOU
PETE: GOODBYE EMILY IN   LONDON WE WISH WE COULD OTALK TO YOU GOODBYE KATY BE BRAVE THINGS WILL CHNGE
JODIE: AND GOODBYE SIX LETTERS SIX YEARS MAYBE ONE DAY YOULL MEET HIM
PETE: GOODBYE MY SON LUVE PLEASE DONT GROW AS CYNIC AL AS YOUR MOTHER
JODIE: GOODBYE MICHEAL COLLINS PLEASE DONT BE LONELY

PETE: GOODBYE JANET AND STEPHEN HAPPY ANNIVERSARY STICK BY EACH OTHER
JODIE: AND OVER HERE THE WIND ON MY FACE IS THE SAME WIND ON YOUR BACK AND OVER HERE WELL NEVER STOP LOVING YOU
PETE: AND WN THE BRIDGE WE SAY GOODBYE OLD FRIENDS OLD CATS MOTHERS IN NEW CASTLE AND FAMILIES IN KENYA
JODIE: AND GOOD LUCK BEAR GOOD LUCK LINDA AND SIMON I HOPE YOU FIND ELLA
PETE: GOODBYE MESSAGES IN FOTTLES AND THE NATIONAL EXPRESS
JODIE: AND I SAY ENOUGH NOW IM TIRED GOODBYE ARM ACHE GOODBYE SORE EYES GOODBYE SHIVERING COME WARM ME UP
PETE: NOT LONG NOW KEEP GOING KEEP WAVING YOUR FLAGS ILL SEE YOU SOON. JODIES ACHING GRMS AND WODIES SORE EYES
JODIE: AND I HOPE NOTHINGS CHANGED I HOPE YOULL STILL LOVE ME
PETE: I HOPE SO TOO EVERY THE ON THE BRIDGE HOPES TOIS ENDS) WELL
JODIE: AND AT THE FOUNTAINS WE SHOUT HELLO FIREWORKS HELLO MARCHING BAND HELLO MY LOVED ONE
PETE: AND WN THE BRIDGE WERE PREPARING FOR THE LONG EMBRKE THE LAST GOODBYE AND THE CHANPAGNE
JODIE: AND I SAY ILL NEVER EVER FORGET YOU
PETE: GOODBYE FOUNTAINS
JODIE: ILL SEE YOU SOON

Day 11: Sunday 15ᵗʰ May 2011

Pete: Here we are.

Jodie: For a while there I thought we'd never make it. → 120 minutes

Pete: We made it, and in two hours well's stop waving these flags.

Jodie: Yes but for the people at the fountains it wont be over.

Pete: Tomorrow there will be a space on this bridge where I have been, but there are so many messages here.

Jodie: And at the fountains we shout goodbye pero, goodbye that bridge, goodbye Ill never forget you.

Pete: And on the bridge we say goodbye eleven long days, goodbye fountains, goodbye the wind at my back.

Jodie: Goodbye baby I carried for seven weeks, goodbye Grandad in heaven, goodbye Karenzza well miss you. → 264 hours

Pete: Goodbye Emily in (London), we wish we could talk to you goodbye Katy be brave, things will change. 118·8 miles / 2hrs 14mins / car

Jodie: And goodbye six letters, six years, maybe one day youll meet him.

Pete: Goodbye my son Luke please dont ever grow as cynical as your mother.

Jodie: Goodbye Michael Collins, please dont be lonely.

Pete: Goodbye Janet and Stephen, happy anniversary, stick by each other.

Jodie: And over here the wind on my face is the same wind on your back and over here well never stop loving you.

Pete: And on the bridge we say goodbye old friends, old cats, mothers in New castle, and families in (Kenya.) 8hrs 36mins / 4300 miles / air

246 miles 5hrs 3mins (car)

Jodie: And goodluck Bear, good luck Simon and Linda, I hope you find Ella. Linda Simon

Pete: Goodbye messages in bottles and the National Express.

Jodie: And I say enough now Im tired, goodbye arm ache, goodbye sore eyes, goodbye shivers, come warm me up.

Pete: Not long now. Keep going. Keep waving your flags, Ill see you soon Jodies aching arms and Jodies sore eyes.

Jodie: And I hope nothings changed, I hope you still love me.

Pete: I hope so too. Every one on the bridge hopes this ends well.

Jodie: And at the fountains we shout hello fireworks, hello marching band, hello my loved ones,

Pete: And on the bridge were preparing for the long embrace, the last goodbye, and the champagne.

Jodie: And I say Ill never ever forget you.

Pete: Goodbye fountains.

Jodie: Ill see you soon.

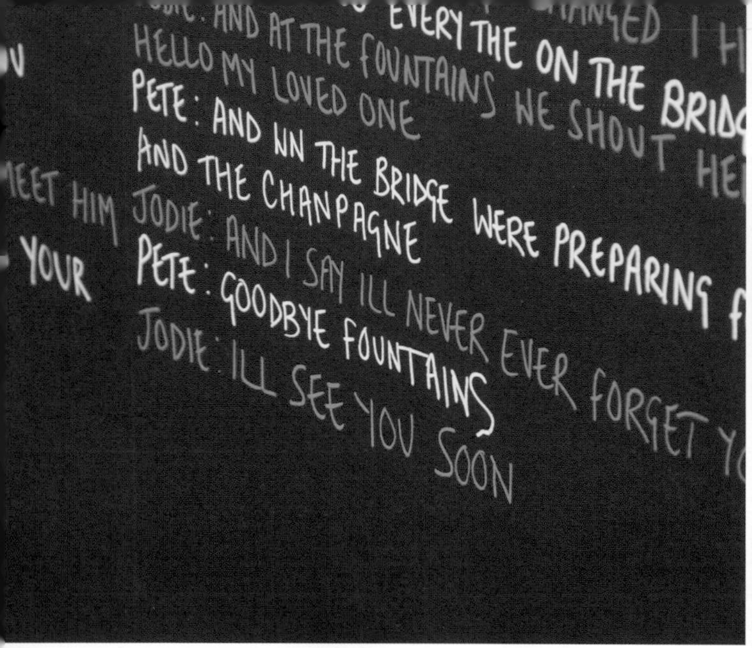
AND AT THE FOUNTAINS WE SHOUT
HELLO MY LOVED ONE
WERE PREPARING
AND THE CHANPAGNE
JODIE: AND I SAY ILL NEVER EVER
YOUR
PETE: GOODBYE FOUNTAINS
JODIE: ILL SEE YOU SOON

END-OF-DAY

- "It is the final day today!!".

- "Bristol 10K day – arrived in town. Took 20 minutes to cross a road. No chance to set up *Save Me*. Everyone unsure, start later, not start? Big decisions!".

- "A lovely way to end the piece. A woman passed extremely excited to see the piece, had not had a chance as she works over 11am-1pm so starting at 2pm meant she got to see it and had heard loads about it".

- "I cried as, now, there are just messages on yellow tags – never going to be any more".

- "Very quiet. A Chinese band turned up – drumming. I cried at the end".

- "Girls on boat under bridge 'Hello flag man', then went back under the bridge "Flag man, do you remember us?".

- "Remember your socks. Lots of dogs today. Reading own message aloud to another – emotional".

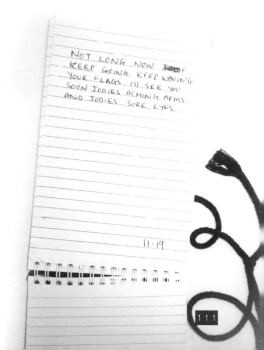

115

SECTION 3:
TAGS

And now we have these tags, personal offerings by people passing by.

The words and stories that have contributed to and defined a rich and varied conversation about separation. As the tags accumulated, Jodie's and Pete's responsibilities shifted. And what started as a domestic conversation between a pair of real-life partners, became a dialogue infused with the voices of a community reflecting on the nature of separateness. Read them for yourself.

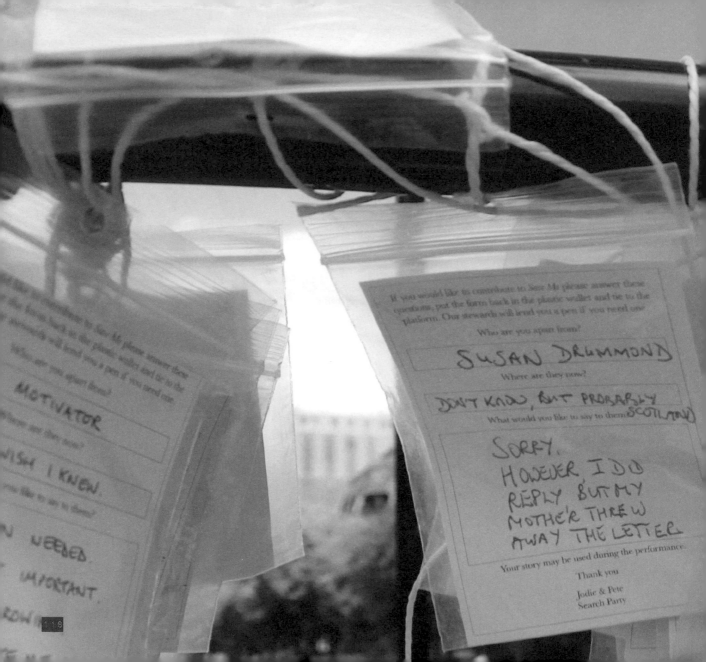

If you would like to contribute to *See Me* please answer these questions, put the form back in the plastic wallet and tie to the platform. Our stewards will lend you a pen if you need one.

Who are you apart from?

SUSAN DRUMMOND

Where are they now?

DON'T KNOW, BUT PROBABLY SCOTLAND

What would you like to say to them?

**SORRY.
HOWEVER, I DO
REPLY BUT MY
MOTHER THREW
AWAY THE LETTER**

Your story may be used during the performance.

Thank you

Jodie & Pete
Search Party

MOTIVATOR

WISH I KNEW.

NEEDED.

IMPORTANT.

118

PETE'S TAGS:
PERO'S BRIDGE

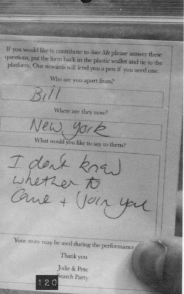

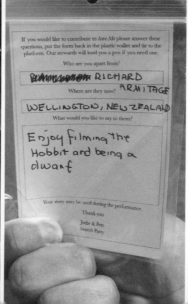

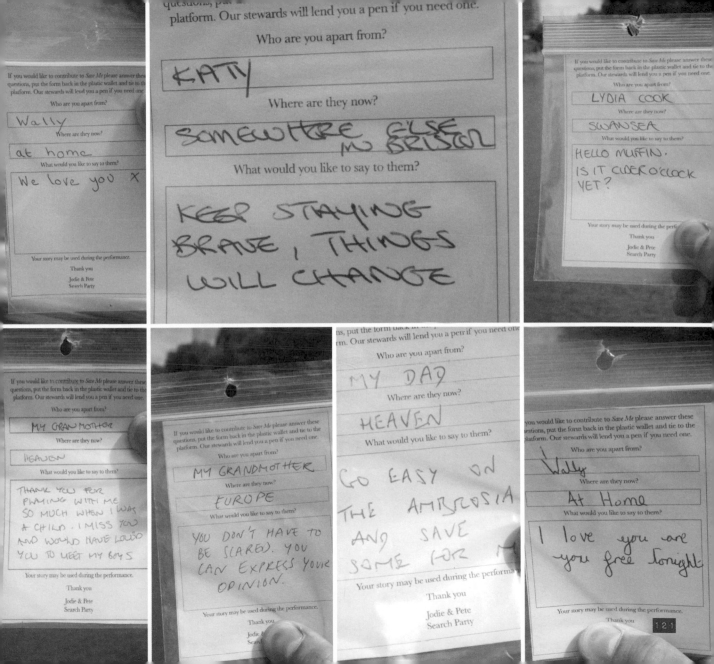

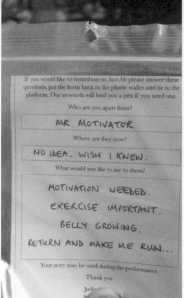

If you would like to contribute to *Save Me* please answer these questions, put the form back in the plastic wallet and tie to the platform. Our stewards will lend you a pen if you need one.

Who are you apart from?

MR MOTIVATOR

Where are they now?

NO IDEA. WISH I KNEW.

What would you like to say to them?

MOTIVATION NEEDED.
EXERCISE IMPORTANT.
BELLY GROWING.
RETURN AND MAKE ME RUN...

Your story may be used during the performance.

Thank you

Jodie & Pete
Search Party

If you would like to contribute to *Save Me* please answer these questions, put the form back in the plastic wallet and tie to the platform. Our stewards will lend you a pen if you need one.

Who are you apart from?

NIMA & MEHRAVEH

Where are they now?

IRAN

What would you like to say to them?

Nima & Mehraveh are separated from their mother, Nasrin Sotoudeh. Nasrin is in prison (since Sept 10). She is a political prisoner, she fights for the rights of other children but is separated from her own. If you read this, think of her children, send the messages, send them hope. Find NASRIN SOTOUDEH on Facebook

Your story may be used during the performance.

Thank you

Jodie & Pete
Search Party

If you would like to contribute to *Save Me* please answer these questions, put the form back in the plastic wallet and tie to the platform. Our stewards will lend you a pen if you need one.

Who are you apart from?

DADDY

Where are they now?

ON WAY TO LONDON.

What would you like to say to them?

WE MISS YOU.
COME HOME
SOON.
XXX

Your story may be used during the performa

Thank you

Jodie & Pete
Search Party

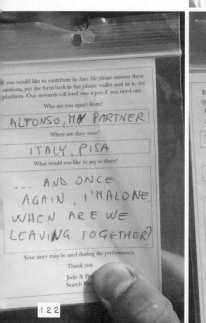

If you would like to contribute to *Save Me* please answer these questions, put the form back in the plastic wallet and tie to the platform. Our stewards will lend you a pen if you need one.

Who are you apart from?

ALFONSO, MY PARTNER

Where are they now?

ITALY, PISA

What would you like to say to them?

... AND ONCE
AGAIN, I'M ALONE.
WHEN ARE WE
LEAVING TOGETHER?

Your story may be used during the performance.

Thank you

Jodie & Pete
Search Party

If you would like to contribute to *Save Me* please answer these questions, put the form back in the plastic wallet and tie to the platform. Our stewards will lend you a pen if you need one.

Who are you apart from?

Dear Friend PAM Dunce

Where are they now?

In Heaven.

What would you like to say to them?

Miss you and
send our
Love
God Bless

Your story may be used during the performance.

Thank you

Jodie & Pete
Search Party

---

platform. Our stewards will lend you a pen

Who are you apart from?

BUSTER

Where are they now?

IN HIS DREAMS

What would you like to say to them?

ENJOY ALL THE
PLACES YOU GO +
FANTASTICAL
CREATERES U MEET.

Your story may be used during the performance.

Thank you

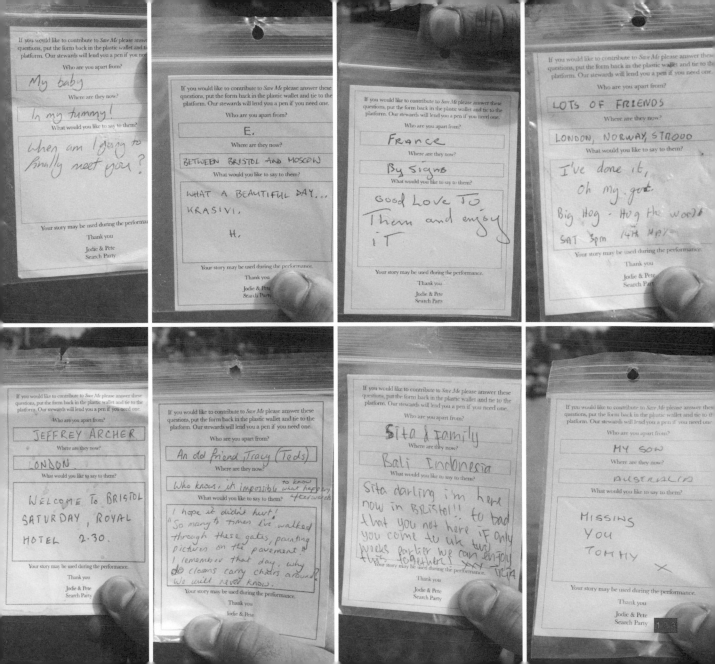

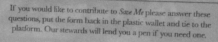

If you would like to contribute to *Save Me* please answer these questions, put the form back in the plastic wallet and tie to the platform. Our stewards will lend you a pen if you need one.

Who are you apart from?

Alice, My 21-yr-old cat.

Where are they now?

San Francisco

What would you like to say to them?

I'm sorry I left you, I love you more than anything. Please be alive when I get home. - Steve
(she wouldn't hear me, because she is deaf. And a cat.)

Your story may be used during the performance.

Thank you

Jodie & Pete
Search Party

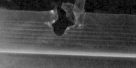

Who are you apart from

DADDY

Where are they now

IN THE GARAGE

What would you like to say t

BOO!

Your story may be used during the p

Thank you

Jodie & Pete
Search Party

If you would like to contribute to *Save Me* please answer these questions, put the form back in the plastic wallet and tie to the platform. Our stewards will lend you a pen if you need one.

Who are you apart from?

RACHEL, SARAH AND GAIL

Where are they now?

BRISTOL, LONDON AND OXFORD

What would you like to say to them?

WHATEVER YOU MAY DO, WHEREVER YOU ARE WITH, WHEREVER YOU MAY ROAM YOU ARE ALWAYS LOVED MUM AND DAD

Your story may be used during the performance.

Thank you

Jodie & Pete
Search Party

If you would like to contribute to *Save Me* please answer these questions, put the form back in the plastic wallet and tie to the platform. Our stewards will lend you a pen if you need one.

Who are you apart from?

NATALIE

Where are they now?

HENDERSONVILLE, NC, USA

What would you like to say to them?

NO DRINKING WITH YOUR SISTER BEFORE 12:00!

Your story may be used during the performance.

Thank you

Jodie & Pete
Search Party

If you would like to contribute to *Save Me* please answer these questions, put the form back in the plastic wallet and tie to the platform. Our stewards will lend you a pen if you need one.

Who are you apart from?

The old us, before 2 lovely babies

Where are they now?

I can still see them in old photographs

What would you like to say to them?

Don't give up the hope. Let's not forget who we were. Look at the photographs. It will get easier. I still love you.

Your story may be used during the performance.

Thank you

Jodie & Pete
Search Party

If you would like to contribute to *Save Me* please answer these questions, put the form back in the plastic wallet and tie to the platform. Our stewards will lend you a pen if you need one.

Who are you apart from?

THE VILLAGERS

Where are they now?

BORNEO

What would you like to say to them?

THANK YOU ALL FOR KEEPING SHAUN SAFE + WELL, WHILE HE WAS WITH YOU FOR 4 MONTHS. AS I HOLD HIS HAND I KNOW THAT YOU ARE HOLDING HIS HEART ♥

Your story may be used during the performance.

Thank you

Jodie & Pete
Search Party

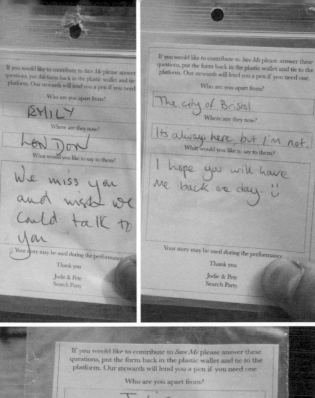

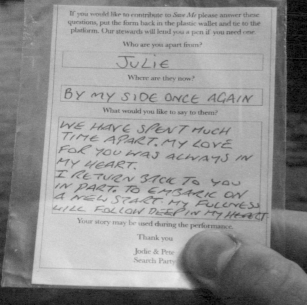

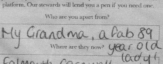

PETE'S TAGS:
PERO'S BRIDGE

If you would like to contribute to *Save Me* please answer these questions, put the form back in the plastic wallet and tie to the platform. Our stewards will lend you a pen if you need one.

Who are you apart from?

MY HUSBAND

Where are they now?

WITH JODIE

What would you like to say to them?

~~STAY~~ CATCH THE NEXT FERRY TO NOVA SCOTIA RACE YA HOME

Your story may be used during the performance.

Thank you

Jodie & Pete
Search Party

If you would like to contribute to *Save Me* please answer these questions, put the form back in the plastic wallet and tie to the platform. Our stewards will lend you a pen if you need one.

Who are you apart from?

MY mum

Where are they now?

NEWCASTLE

What would you like to say to them?

I WISH WE LIVED CLOSE ENOUGH TO POP IN FOR A CUP OF TEA - SOMETHING SMALL INSTEAD OF ALL OR NOTHING - AND I WOULD FEEL LIKE A BETTER DAUGHTER

Your story may be used during the performance.

Thank you

Jodie & Pete
Search Party

If you would like to contribute to *Save Me* please answer these questions, put the form back in the plastic wallet and tie to the platform. Our stewards will lend you a pen if you need one.

Who are you apart from?

SHAUN

Where are they now?

HOLDING MY HAND

What would you like to say to them?

I FEEL YOUR HAND AS WE STAND. SO STRONG + WARM. NOW I WAIT FOR YOUR HEART TO RETURN FROM BORNEO

Your story may be used during the performance.

Thank you

Jodie & Pete
Search Party

If you would like to contribute to *Save Me* please answer these questions, put the form back in the plastic wallet and tie to the platform. Our stewards will lend you a pen if you need one.

Who are you apart from?

Sandra

Where are they now?

Greifswald, Germany

What would you like to say to them?

One year ago you were just beginning your Bristol adventures, now you are home trischity. Will not forget you.

Your story may be used during the performance.

126 Thank you

Jodie & Pete
Search Party

If you would like to contribute to *Save Me* please answer these questions, put the form back in the plastic wallet and tie to the platform. Our stewards will lend you a pen if you need one.

Who are you apart from?

LAB

Where are they now?

CLEANING THE FLAT

What would you like to say to them?

I WOULD MARRY YOU IN A SECOND BUT I CANT AFFORD A RING — BEAR x

Your story may be used during the performance.

Thank you

Jodie & Pete
Search Party

If you would like to contribute to *Save Me* please answer these questions, put the form back in the plastic wallet and tie to the platform. Our stewards will lend you a pen if you need one.

Who are you apart from?

My son, Luke

Where are they now?

With his father - somewhere...

What would you like to say to them?

Life is a glorious cycle of song A medley of extemporanea. Please don't ever grow as cynical as your mother.

Your story may be used during the performance.

Thank you

Jodie & Pete
Search Party

If you would like to contribute to *Save Me* please answer these questions, put the form back in the plastic wallet and tie to the platform. Our stewards will lend you a pen if you need one.

Who are you apart from?

TOM & PIP

Where are they now?

IN A FIELD

What would you like to say to them?

EOR EOR & HE ALWAYS CALLS ME DONKEY!

Your story may be used during the performance.

Thank you

Jodie & Pete
Search Party

Form 1

If you would like to contribute to *Save Me* please answer these questions, put the form back in the plastic wallet and tie to the platform. Our stewards will lend you a pen if you need one.

Who are you apart from?

TOADY

Where are they now?

AT HOME

What would you like to say to them?

KEEP DRY

Your story may be used during the performance.

Thank you

Jodie & Pete
Search Party

Form 2

If you would like to contribute to *Save Me* please answer these questions, put the form back in the plastic wallet and tie to the platform. Our stewards will lend you a pen if you need one.

Who are you apart from?

My boyfriend

Where are they now?

in Oxford

What would you like to say to them?

I know (I hope) I will see you tonight but last night I was in a hotel room in Bristol, wandering streets before that, sleeping on one side of the bed, so that if you come there would be space. For you

Your story may be used during the performance.

Thank you

Jodie & Pete
Search Party

Form 3

If you would like to contribute to *Save Me* please answer these questions, put the form back in the plastic wallet and tie to the platform. Our stewards will lend you a pen if you need one.

Who are you apart from?

My family

Where are they now?

across the sea

What would you like to say to them?

We are hundreds of miles apart + I dont know when I'll see you again!

Your story may be used during the performance.

Thank you

Form 4

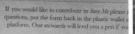

If you would like to contribute to *Save Me* please answer these questions, put the form back in the plastic wallet and tie to the platform. Our stewards will lend you a pen if you need one.

Who are you apart from?

THE OTHER FLAG

Where are they now?

OVER THERE

What would you like to say to them?

JUST BECAUSE RED AND YELLOW MAKES YOU SALIVATE DONT GO MACCY D!

Your story may be used during the performance.

Thank you

Jodie & Pete
Search Party

Form 5

If you would like to contribute to *Save Me* please answer these questions, put the form back in the plastic wallet and tie to the platform. Our stewards will lend you a pen if you need one.

Who are you apart from?

Squeak

Where are they now?

At home on the sofa

What would you like to say to them?

We hope you're not catching anything. Jean does not like the headless rats We love you squeaky

Your story may be used during the performance.

Thank you

Jodie & Pete
Search Party

Form 6

If you would like to contribute to *Save Me* please answer these questions, put the form back in the plastic wallet and tie to the platform. Our stewards will lend you a pen if you need one.

Who are you apart from?

My Dad

Where are they now?

In Eastington

What would you like to say to them?

You don't know what you're m...

Your story may be used during the performance.

Thank you

Jodie & Pete
Search Party

Form 7

If you would like to contribute to *Save Me* please answer these questions, put the form back in the plastic wallet and tie to the platform. Our stewards will lend you a pen if you need one.

Who are you apart from?

I'm Joanne.

Where are they now?

From France

What would you like to say to them?

Bristol is a nice city! Très jolie ville! Des baises.

Your story may be used during the performance.

Thank you

Jodie & Pete
Search Party

If you would like to contribute to *Save Me* please answer these questions, put the form back in the plastic wallet and tie to the platform. Our stewards will lend you a pen if you need one.

Who are you apart from?

Ieuan e Owen

Where are they now?

In bed.

What would you like to say to them?

Get up and revise. WOW!

Your story may be used during the performance.

Thank you

Jodie & Pete
Search Party

If you would like to contribute to *Save Me* please answer these questions, put the form back in the plastic wallet and tie to the platform. Our stewards will lend you a pen if you need one.

Who are you apart from?

Where are they now?

What would you like to say to them?

HI TO THE GIRL WHO
EXPLAINED SP TO ME
YESTERDAY

Your story may be used during the performance.

Thank you

Jodie & Pete
Search Party

If you would like to contribute to *Save Me* please answer these questions, put the form back in the plastic wallet and tie to the platform. Our stewards will lend you a pen if you need one.

Who are you apart from?

LEISA

Where are they now?

ELSEWHERE.

What would you like to say to them?

THANK YOU FOR
EVERYTHING YOU
LEFT US WITH.
AND YOU WILL NEVER
LEAVE US.

Your story may be used during the performance.

Thank you

Jodie & Pete
Search Party

If you would like to contribute to *Save Me* please answer these questions, put the form back in the plastic wallet and tie to the platform. Our stewards will lend you a pen if you need one.

Who are you apart from?

SANDRINE

Where are they now?

IN HER JOB

What would you like to say to them?

It's been a great
experience stay with
you. We'd like to
repeat it soon/our best tours
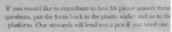
Your story may be used during the performance. guide
the
all of

Thank you

Jodie & Pete
Search Party

If you would like to contribute to *Save Me* please answer these questions, put the form back in the plastic wallet and tie to the platform. Our stewards will lend you a pen if you need one.

Who are you apart from?

KAY.

Where are they now?

PASSED AWAY

What would you like to say to them?

LONG LOST
SORELY MISSED
NEVER FORGOTTEN
LIVING ON

Your story may be used during the performance.

Thank you

Jodie & Pete
Search Party

Our stewards will lend you a pen if you need...

Who are you apart from?

RORY

Where are they now?

NO LONGER HERE

What would you like to say to them?

How could you be so stupid? I miss you.

Your story may be used during the performance.

Thank...

Jo...
S...

If you would like to contribute to *Save Me* please answer these questions, put the form back in the plastic wallet and tie to the platform. Our stewards will lend you a pen if you need one.

Who are you apart from?

Ooter

Where are they now?

The big Smoke

What would you like to say to them?

your baby boy is beautiful and I am looking forward to meeting him. love you lots.

Your story may be used during the performance.

Thank you

Jodie & Pete
Search Party

If you would like to contribute to *Save Me* please answer these questions, put the form back in the plastic wallet and tie to the platform. Our stewards will lend you a pen if you need one.

Who are you apart from?

Rosie & Declan

Where are they now?

USA

What would you like to say to them?

Meet you in New York for Bagels.

Your story may be used during the performance.

Thank you

Jodie & Pete
Search Party

If you would like to contribute to *Save Me* please answer these questions, put the form back in the plastic wallet and tie to the platform. Our stewards will lend you a pen if you need one.

Who are you apart from?

PERSEPHONE

Where are they now?

ETERNITY

What would you like to say to them?

I CARRIED YOU FOR 7 WEEKS. I WISH THAT YOU WERE HERE WITH ME. I WILL BE A BRAVER PERSON FOR CONCEIVING YOU.

Your story may be used during the performance.

Thank you

Jodie & Pete
Search Party

---

questions, put the form back in the plastic wallet and tie to the platform. Our stewards will lend you a pen if you need one.

Who are you apart from?

LEON

Where are they now?

IN BED

What would you like to say to them?

SEE YOU TONIGHT

#1 SON

LOVE MUMMY AND BEN X

Your story may be used during the performance.

Thank you

Jodie & Pete
Search Party 129

If you would like to contribute to *Save Me* please answer these questions, put the form back in the plastic wallet and tie to the platform. Our stewards will lend you a pen if you need one.

Who are you apart from?

mum + dad

Where are they now?

Pennsylvania, USA

What would you like to say to them?

Hurry up + book a flight to come and see us in Bristol soon! your grandson is growing fast!!

Your story may be used **during the performance.**

Thank you

Jo
S

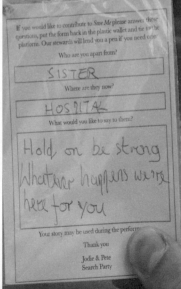

platform. Our stewards will lend you a pen if you need

Who are you apart from?

My sister in law

Where are they now?

What would you like to say to them?

It is not your fault Don't feel guilty.

If you would like to contribute to *Save Me* please answer these questions, put the form back in the plastic wallet and tie to the platform. Our stewards will lend you a pen if you need one.

Who are you apart from?

MY FRIEND

Where are they now?

SUFFOLK

What would you like to say to them?

WHY DON'T YOU COME BACK AND BE WITH US HERE? DON'T BE ALONE

Your story may be used during the performance.

130

Thank you

Jodie & Pete
Search Party

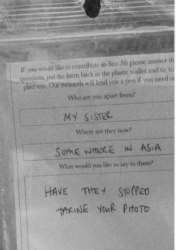

If you would like to contribute to *Save Me* please answer th questions, put the form back in the plastic wallet and tie to platform. Our stewards will lend you a pen if you need or

Who are you apart from?

MY SISTER

Where are they now?

SOME WHERE IN ASIA

What would you like to say to them?

HAVE THEY STOPPED TAKING YOUR PHOTO

Your story may be used during the performance.

Thank you

Jodie
Sea

If you would like to contribute to *Save Me* please answer these questions, put the form back in the plastic wallet and tie to the platform. Our stewards will lend you a pen if you need one.

Who are you apart from?

SISTER

Where are they now?

HOSPITAL

What would you like to say to them?

Hold on be strong Whatever happens we're here for you

Your story may be used during the performe

Thank you

Jodie & Pete
Search Party

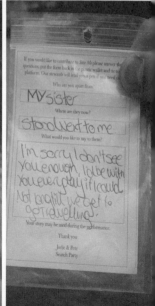

If you would like to contribute to *Save Me* please answer the questions, put the form back in the plastic wallet and tie to platform. Our stewards will lend you a pen if you need

Who are you apart from?

MY sister

Where are they now?

Stood next to me

What would you like to say to them?

I'm sorry I don't see you enough, I'd be with you everyday if I could. Not long till we get to go travelling.

Your story may be used during the performance.

Thank you

Jodie & Pete
Search Party

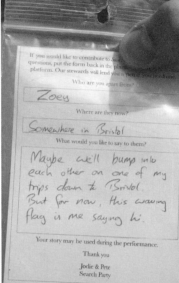
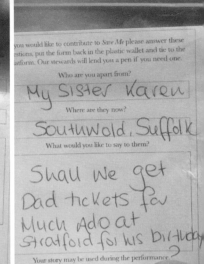

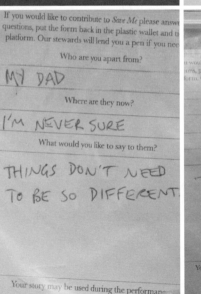
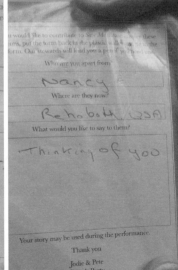

JODIE'S TAGS:
FOUNTAIN STEPS

If you would like to contribute to *Save Me* please answer these questions, put the form back in the plastic wallet and tie to the platform. Our stewards will lend you a pen if you need one.

Who are you apart from?

MUMMY-MUMMY · DADDY

Where are they now?

crispins wedding

What would you like to say to them?

dear My Mum and Dad we MissedYou ++tooKoXoXo

Your story may be used during the performance.

Thank you

Jodie & Pete
Search Party

If you would like to contribute to *Save Me* please answer these questions, put the form back in the plastic wallet and tie to the platform. Our stewards will lend you a pen if you need one.

Who are you apart from?

Family and Friends

Where are they now?

Belgium

What would you like to say to them?

I'm coming Home After 3 years of Separation. Love you ALL

Your story may be used during the performance.

Thank you

Jodie & Pete
Search Party

---

uld like to contribute to *Save Me* please answer these put the form back in the plastic wallet and tie to the Our stewards will lend you a pen if you need one.

Who are you apart from?

MORGAN

Where are they now?

CANADA

What would you like to say to them?

ARE YOU FEELING BETTER?

Your story may be used during the performance.

Thank you

Jodie & Pete
Search Party

If you would like to contribute to *Save Me* please answer these questions, put the form back in the plastic wallet and tie to the platform. Our stewards will lend you a pen if you need one.

Who are you apart from?

Katie - my big sister

Where are they now?

on an adventure around the world!

What would you like to say to them?

I sort of miss you — but don't want to admit it to your face. (and I stole your shoes)

Thank you

Jodie & Pete
Search Party

If you would like to contribute to *Save Me* please answer these questions, put the form back in the plastic wallet and tie to the platform. Our stewards will lend you a pen if you need one.

Who are you apart from?

LONDON & MONTREAL

Where are they now?

MONTREAL

What would you like to say to them?

ALL OUR LOVE TO MARION JOHN MANDY, MATT & FAMILY THINKING OF YOU ALL xxx

Your story may be used during the performance.

Thank you

Jodie & Pete
Search Party

If you would like to contribute to *Save Me* please answer these questions, put the form back in the plastic wallet and tie to the platform. Our stewards will lend you a pen if you need one.

Who are you apart from?

Red Neck, Norton

Where are they now?

L.A.

What would you like to say to them?

To many why's to many Reason. to far apart..

Your story may be used during the performance.

Thank you

Jodie & Pete
Search Party

---

ould like to contribute to *Save Me* please answer these questions, put the form back in the plastic wallet and tie to the platform. Our stewards will lend you a pen if you need one.

Who are you apart from?

My Parents

Where are they now?

Groningen, the Netherlands

What would you like to say to them?

I'm looking forward to seeing you again in the summer. Thank you for all your support.

Your story may be used during the performance.

Thank you

Jodie & Pete
Search Party

If you would like to contribute to *Save Me* please answer these questions, put the form back in the plastic wallet and tie to the platform. Our stewards will lend you a pen if you need one.

Who are you apart from?
My Mum and Dad

Where are they now?
Bahrain

What would you like to say to them?
Thankyou for all you've done. And all that you do for me. XX

Your story may be used during the performance.

Thank you

Jodie & Pete
Search Party

---

platform. Our stewards will...

Who are you apart from?
~~KATEN~~ KARENZZA

Where are they now?
CORNWAL / HEAVEN

What would you like to say to them?
I MISS YOU EVERY DAY AND WISH YOU weren't taken From ME AFTER I (FOUND) you AGAIN.

...may be used during the performance.

If you would like to contribute to *Save Me* please answer these questions, put the form back in the plastic wallet and tie to the platform. Our stewards will lend you a pen if you need one.

Who are you apart from?
MY BROTHER ANDY

Where are they now?
SPAIN

What would you like to say to them?
YOU SHOULD COME TO MY WEDDING. YOU LIVE LIKE A HERMIT. I MISS YOU

Your story may be used during the performance.

Thank you

Jodie & Pete
Search Party

If you would like to contribute to *Save Me* please answer these questions, put the form back in the plastic wallet and tie to the platform. Our stewards will lend you a pen if you need one.

Who are you apart from?
MY GRANDAD

Where are they now?
IN A BETTER PLACE

What would you like to say to them?
You still have an influence on me

Your story may be used during the performance.

Thank you

Jodie & Pete
Search Party

---

you would like to contribute to *Save Me* please answer these questions, put the form back in the plastic wallet and tie to the platform. Our stewards will lend you a pen if you need one.

Who are you apart from?
Mark

Where are they now?
the other side of death

What would you like to say to them?
Are you still dancing? I still miss you

Your story may be used during the performance.

Thank you

Jodie & Pete
Search Party

If you would like to contribute to *Save Me* please answer these questions, put the form back in the plastic wallet and tie to the platform. Our stewards will lend you a pen if you need one.

Who are you apart from?
NEMO

Where are they now?
IN THE SEA SOMEWHERE

What would you like to say to them?
WHERE ARE YOU? OH THERE YOU ARE, NEVERMIND!

Your story may be used during the performance.

Thank you

Jodie & Pete
Search Party

questions, put the form back in ... platform. Our stewards will lend you a pen if you need one.

Who are you apart from?

My Dog

Where are they now?

Cremated

What would you like to say to them?

I love you x

If you would like to contribute to *Save Me* please answer these questions, put the form back in the plastic wallet and tie to the platform. Our stewards will lend you a pen if you need one.

Who are you apart from?

OUR CHILDREN FOR CERTAIN REASONS

Where are they now?

EVERYWHERE

What would you like to say to them?

NO MATTER WHERE YOU ARE AND WHAT YOU ARE DOING, WE ALWAYS WANT YOU TO KNOW WE ARE THERE

Your story may be used during the performance.

Thank you

Jodie & Pete
Search Party

If you would like to contribute to *Save Me* please answer these questions, put the form back in the plastic wallet and tie to the platform. Our stewards will lend you a pen if you need one.

Who are you apart from?

The mr that is doing exactly ...

Where are they now?

Hopefully up ahead

What would you like to say to them?

Can you give me some directions - I can't find you, It's foggy

Your story may be used during the performance.

Thank you

Jodie & Pete
Search Party

If you would like to contribute to *Save Me* please answer these questions, put the form back in the plastic wallet and tie to the platform. Our stewards will lend you a pen if you need one.

Who are you apart from?

MO

Where are they now?

France

What would you like to say to them?

"Walk them bush"

Your story may be used during the performance.

Thank you

Jodie & Pete
Search Party

If you would like to contribute to *Save Me* please answer these questions, put the form back in the plastic wallet and tie to the platform. Our stewards will lend you a pen if you need one.

Who are you apart from?

My sister

Where are they now?

In sydney

What would you like to say to them?

come back to us when your heart is mended

Your story may be used during the performance.

Thank you

Jodie & Pete
Search Party

If you would like to contribute to *Save Me* please answer these questions, put the form back in the plastic wallet and tie to the platform. Our stewards will lend you a pen if you need one.

Who are you apart from?

LIZZY

Where are they now?

Bournemouth

What would you like to say to them?

Hope you have a good time! Please travel home safely! x

Your story may be used during the performance.

Thank you

Jodie & Pete
Search Party

Card 1

If you would like to contribute to *Save Me* please answer these questions, put the form back in the plastic wallet and tie to the platform. Our stewards will lend you a pen if you need one.

Who are you apart from?

Mother

Where are they now?

Devon

What would you like to say to them?

I'm moving to London

Your story may be used during the performance.

Thank you

Jodie & Pete
Search Party

Card 2

If you would like to contribute to *Save Me* please answer these questions, put the form back in the plastic wallet and tie to the platform. Our stewards will lend you a pen if you need one.

Who are you apart from?

My boyfriend

Where are they now?

Spain

What would you like to say to them?

I'm waiting for you, love.
You are always in my thoughts.
see you in 2 weeks!!

Your story may be used during the performance.

Thank you

Jodie & Pete
Search Party

Card 3

If you would like to contribute to *Save Me* please answer these questions, put the form back in the plastic wallet and tie to the platform. Our stewards will lend you a pen if you need one.

Who are you apart from?

My grandad

Where are they now?

in hevan

What would you like to say to them?

I MISS you and evan though we wern't that close i still loves you
XXXXXX

Your story may be used during the performance.

Thank you

Jodie & Pete
Search Party

Card 4

If you would like to contribute to *Save Me* please answer these questions, put the form back in the plastic wallet and tie to the platform. Our stewards will lend you a pen if you need one.

Who are you apart from?

My Father

Where are they now?

New Zealand

What would you like to say to them?

I want to talk to you again, To patch things up. It's been so long. I miss you.

Your story may be used during the performance.

Thank you

Jodie & Pete
Search Party

Card 5

If you would like to contribute to *Save Me* please answer these questions, put the form back in the plastic wallet and tie to the platform. Our stewards will lend you a pen if you need one.

Who are you apart from?

FAILURE

Where are they now?

IN THE PAST

What would you like to say to them?

IT FEELS STRANGE to MISS FAILURE, NOW WE'VE WON SOMETHING

Your story may be used during the performance.

Thank you

Jodie & Pete
Search Party

Card 6

If you would like to contribute to *Save Me* please answer these questions, put the form back in the plastic wallet and tie to the platform. Our stewards will lend you a pen if you need one.

Who are you apart from?

MY DAD

Where are they now?

DURHAM

What would you like to say to them?

I KNOW YOU MISS US, BUT WE LOVE YOU SO MUCH. HAPPY BIRTHDAY

Your story may be used during the performance.

Thank you

Jodie & Pete
Search Party

Card 7

If you would like to contribute to *Save Me* please answer these questions, put the form back in the plastic wallet and tie to the platform. Our stewards will lend you a pen if you need one.

Who are you apart from?

My Nanny Josie

Where are they now?

heaven

What would you like to say to them?

I love you Nan you were the Best and still are FROM TIERAN

Your story may be used during the performance.

Thank you

Jodie & Pete
Search Party

Card 8

If you would like to contribute to *Save Me* please answer these questions, put the form back in the plastic wallet and tie to the platform. Our stewards will lend you a pen if you need one.

Who are you apart from?

No One

Where are they now?

with me

What would you like to say to them?

I love you all

Your story may be used during the performance.

Thank you

Jodie & Pete
Search Party

Form 1:

If you would like to contribute to *Save Me* please answer these questions, put the form back in the plastic wallet and tie to the platform. Our stewards will lend you a pen if you need one.

Who are you apart from?

> MUM

Where are they now?

> NOT ENTIRELY SURE

What would you like to say to them?

> CAN I HAVE THE PAINTING YOU DID OF THE POMEGRANATES PLEASE?

Your story may be used during the performance.

Thank you

Jodie & Pete
Search Party

Form 2:

If you would like to contribute to *Save Me* please answer these questions, put the form back in the plastic wallet and tie to the platform. Our stewards will lend you a pen if you need one.

Who are you apart from?

> My dad

Where are they now?

> AFRICA

What would you like to say to them?

> hope you're having fun, miss + love you lots xxx

Your story may be used during the performance.

Thank you

Jodie & Pete
Search Party

Form 3:

If you would like to contribute to *Save Me* please answer these questions, put the form back in the plastic wallet and tie to the platform. Our stewards will lend you a pen if you need one.

Who are you apart from?

> My family (and my little dog)

Where are they now?

> SPAIN

What would you like to say to them?

> I'm looking forward to seeing you this summer.

Your story may be used during the performance.

Thank you

Jodie & Pete
Search Party

Form 4:

If you would like to contribute to *Save Me* please answer these questions, put the form back in the plastic wallet and tie to the platform. Our stewards will lend you a pen if you need one.

Who are you apart from?

> KAYLA 4 month

Where are they now?

> IN HOSPITAL

What would you like to say to them?

> get well soon Darling miss you From gt grandma

Your story may be used during the performance.

Thank you

Jodie & Pete
Search Party

Form 5:

If you would like to contribute to *Save Me* please answer these questions, put the form back in the plastic wallet and tie to the platform. Our stewards will lend you a pen if you need one.

Who are you apart from?

> Michelle + Nancy + Brandal

Where are they now?

> Check republic / Exeter

What would you like to say to them?

> Hello, how are you I hope your having a good time from nicole. How are you? I hope you having a good time in Exeter Sarah

Your story may be used during the performance.

Thank you

Jodie & Pete
Search Party

Form 6:

If you would like to contribute to *Save Me* please answer these questions, put the form back in the plastic wallet and tie to the platform. Our stewards will lend you a pen if you need one.

Who are you apart from?

> MIRIAM

Where are they now?

> HEAVAN

What would you like to say to them?

> GREETINGS FROM THE HABOURSIDE MUCH LOVE

Your story may be used during the performance.

Thank you

Jodie & Pete
Search Party

Form 7:

If you would like to contribute to *Save Me* please answer these questions, put the form back in the plastic wallet and tie to the platform. Our stewards will lend you a pen if you need one.

Who are you apart from?

> The love of my life

Where are they now?

> In my bed

What would you like to say to them?

> Don't go home x

Your story may be used during the performance.

Thank you

Jodie & Pete
Search Party

Form 1:

If you would like to contribute to *Save Me* please answer these questions, put the form back in the plastic wallet and tie to the platform. Our stewards will lend you a pen if you need one.

Who are you apart from?

ERNIE CUSS

Where are they now?

DORCHESTER

What would you like to say to them?

BRITAIN EXPECTS

Your story may be used during the performance.

Thank you

Jodie & Pete
Search Party

Form 2:

If you would like to contribute to *Save Me* please answer these questions, put the form back in the plastic wallet and tie to the platform. Our stewards will lend you a pen if you need one.

Who are you apart from?

CAPTAIN BIRDSEYE

Where are they now?

LOST @ SEA

What would you like to say to them?

YOU LOST THE MOON WHILST COUNTING THE STARS

Your story may be used during the performance.

www.myspace.com/thedirtyprotestlive

Thank you

Jodie & Pete
Search Party

Form 3:

If you would like to contribute to *Save Me* please answer these questions, put the form back in the plastic wallet and tie to the platform. Our stewards will lend you a pen if you need one.

Who are you apart from?

SARA (MY EX)

Where are they now?

CLEVEDON

What would you like to say to them?

SO YOU ARE MOVING WHY AND WHERE I'M CURIOS AND UNSETTLED

Your story may be used during the performance.

Thank you

Jodie & Pete
Search Party

Form 4:

If you would like to contribute to *Save Me* please answer these questions, put the form back in the plastic wallet and tie to the platform. Our stewards will lend you a pen if you need one.

Who are you apart from?

I'm apart from my gran my Uncle Colin also

Where are they now?

Passed on into other World

What would you like to say to them?

I would like to them boff they are safe now no more suffering they have moved onto the next world. Melanie knows

Your story may be used during the performance.

Thank you

Jodie & Pete
Search Party

Form 5:

If you would like to contribute to *Save Me* please answer these questions, put the form back in the plastic wallet and tie to the platform. Our stewards will lend you a pen if you need one.

Who are you apart from?

Jenny

Where are they now?

Bonnie Scotland

What would you like to say to them?

Have fun with the exams, I left you some marshmallows in the fridge

Your story may be used during the performance.

Thank you

Jodie & Pete
Search Party

Form 6:

you would like to contribute to *Save Me* please answer these questions, put the form back in the plastic wallet and tie to platform. Our stewards will lend you a pen if you need one.

Who are you apart from?

My brother

Where are they now?

Middle East

What would you like to say to them?

rise up

Your story may be used during the perf

Thank you

Jodie & Pete
Search Party

Form 7:

If you would like to contribute to *Save Me* please answer these questions, put the form back in the plastic wallet and tie to the platform. Our stewards will lend you a pen if you need one.

Who are you apart from?

MR KIM

Where are they now?

KOREA

What would you like to say to them?

Thanks for opening my eyes

the performance.

139

If you would like to contribute to *Save Me* please answer these questions, put the form back in the plastic wallet and tie to the platform. Our stewards will lend you a pen if you need one.

Who are you apart from?

MY BOYFRIEND

Where are they now?

WHERE I'M NOT

What would you like to say to them?

**GOOD LUCK MONDAY.
YOU'LL BE GREAT.
MISSING YOU.
NOW LEARN THAT
CATALOGUE! xXx**

Your story may be used during the performance.

Thank you

Jodie & Pete
Search Party

If you would like to contribute to *Save Me* please answer these questions, put the form back in the plastic wallet and tie to the platform. Our stewards will lend you a pen if you need one.

Who are you apart from?

SPAIN ~~~~

Where are they now?

BRISTOL

What would you like to say to them?

~~~~ **Congratulations,
I ~~~~ think that
is a great idea.**

Your story may be used during the performance.

Thank you

Jodie & Pete
Search Party

If you would like to contribute to *Save Me* please answer these questions, put the form back in the plastic wallet and tie to the platform. Our stewards will lend you a pen if you need one.

Who are you apart from?

MY UNCLE BARRY

Where are they now?

FRANCE

What would you like to say to them?

HOW'S IT GOING

Your story may be used during the performance

Thank you

Jodie & Pete
Search Party

If you would like to contribute to *Save Me* please answer these questions, put the form back in the plastic wallet and tie to the platform. Our stewards will lend you a pen if you need one.

Who are you apart from?

Emily & Lee

Where are they now?

Italy

What would you like to say to them?

*I'm so happy for
you both!
Looks like another bridesmaid
dress is on the cards!*

Your story may be used during the performance.

Thank you

Jodie & Pete
Search Party

If you would like to contribute to *Save Me* please answer these questions, put the form back in the plastic wallet and tie to the platform. Our stewards will lend you a pen if you need one.

Who are you apart from?

Mum

Where are they now?

Liverpool

What would you like to say to them?

*I FEAR I WILL NEVER SAY
I LOVE YOU ENOUGH TIMES
BEFORE YOU ARE GONE.*

Your story may be used during the performance.

Thank you

Jodie & Pete
Search Party

If you would like to contribute to *Save Me* please answer these questions, put the form back in the plastic wallet and tie to the platform. Our stewards will lend you a pen if you need one.

Who are you apart from?

GELI

Where are they now?

Bristol = I do live in Germany

What would you like to say to them?

**My lovely Sister,
I ♡ U ♡
~~Too~~ Take care of
you and your baby.
♡ Bruu**

Your story may be used during the performance.

Thank you

Jodie & Pete
Search Party

If you would like to contribute to *Save Me* please answer these questions, put the form back in the plastic wallet and tie to the platform. Our stewards will lend you a pen if you need one.

Who are you apart from?

MY FRIENDS

Where are they now?

AFGHANISTAN

What would you like to say to them?

**PLEASE TAKE
CARE, THINKING OF
YOU ALWAYS.**

Your story may be used during the performance.

Thank you

Jodie & Pete
Search Party

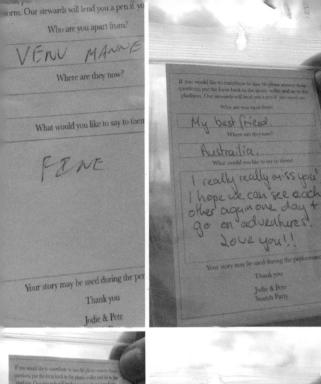

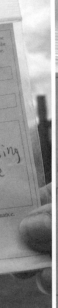
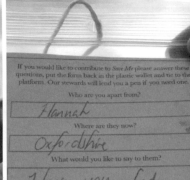

If you would like to contribute to *Save Me* please answer these questions, put the form back in the plastic wallet and tie to the platform. Our stewards will lend you a pen if you need one.

Who are you apart from?

Lynette Tara Kellman – a woman I loved for many years

Where are they now?

Trinidad.

What would you like to say to them?

"You never ever said Goodbye."

Your story may be used during the performance.

Thank you

Jodie & Pete
Search Party

If you would like to contribute to *Save Me* please answer these questions, put the form back in the plastic wallet and tie to the platform. Our stewards will lend you a pen if you need one.

Who are you apart from?

bear

Where are they now?

making a slut

What would you like to say to them?

Happy Anniversary my petit cornichon

Marry me !!!

Your story may be used during the performance.

Thank you

Jodie & Pete
Search Party

If you would like to contribute to *Save Me* please answer these questions, put the form back in the plastic wallet and tie to the platform. Our stewards will lend you a pen if you need one.

Who are you apart from?

Grandma Jean

Where are they now?

I Don't Know

What would you like to say to them?

Thank you for giving is life

Your story may be used during the performance.

Thank you

Jodie & Pete
Search Party

If you would like to contribute to *Save Me* please answer these questions, put the form back in the plastic wallet and tie to the platform. Our stewards will lend you a pen if you need one.

Who are you apart from?

MY SON (PETE)

Where are they now?

CORNWALL DEVON

What would you like to say to them?

Happy Birthday Pete Enjoy the Party and the sunset

Your story may be used during the performance.

Thank you

Jodie & Pete
Search Party

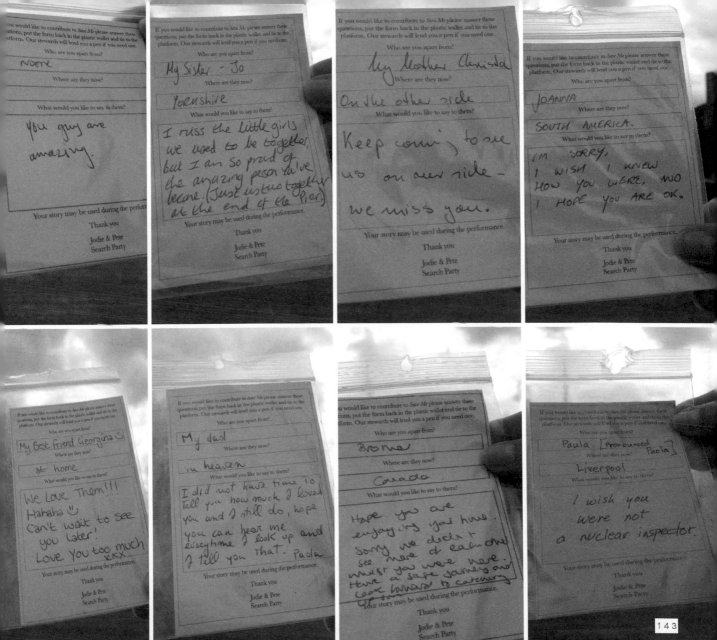

If you would like to contribute to *Save Me* please answer these questions, put the form back in the plastic wallet and tie to the platform. Our stewards will lend you a pen if you need one.

Who are you apart from?

My Son

Where are they now?

Nursery

What would you like to say to them?

I love you so much, it makes me so happy to see you. You're my favourite.

Your story may be used during the performance.

Thank you

Jodie & Pete
Search Party

If you would like to contribute to *Save Me* please answer these questions, put the form back in the plastic wallet and tie to the platform. Our stewards will lend you a pen if you need one.

Who are you apart from?

NICE – FRANCE

Where are they now?

MOUGINS (South France)

What would you like to say to them?

Having a lovely time in Bristol (1st visit) Nice city. good company (Helen & Mark). Bisou. MUM

Your story may be used during the performance.

Thank you

Jodie & Pete
Search Party

If you would like to contribute to *Save Me* please answer these questions, put the form back in the plastic wallet and tie to the platform. Our stewards will lend you a pen if you need one.

Who are you apart from?

OLD STICK (GRANNY)

Where are they now?

DEAD

What would you like to say to them?

UNITED ARE IN THE EUROPEAN CUP FINAL AGAIN!

Your story may be used during the performance.

Thank you

Jodie & Pete
Search Party

If you would like to contribute to *Save Me* please answer these questions, put the form back in the plastic wallet and tie to the platform. Our stewards will lend you a pen if you need one.

Who are you apart from?

R

Where are they now?

I wish I knew

What would you like to say to them?

Hope you're safe & well

Your story may be used during the performance.

Thank you

Jodie & Pete
Search Party

144

If you would like to contribute to *Save Me* please answer these questions, put the form back in the plastic wallet and tie to the platform. Our stewards will lend you a pen if you need one.

Who are you apart from?

MY MUM

Where are they now?

IN CUMBRIA

What would you like to say to them?

I LOVE YOU VERY MUCH AND CAN'T WAIT TO SEE YOU IN TWO WEEKS

Your story may be used during the performance.

Thank you

Jodie & Pete
Search Party

If you would like to contribute to *Save Me* please answer these questions, put the form back in the plastic wallet and tie to the platform. Our stewards will lend you a pen if you need one.

Who are you apart from?

SKYE OUR Dog

Where are they now?

IN KENNELS IN SCOTLAND

What would you like to say to them?

MISSING OUR WALKS ALREADY. BRISTOL IS LOVELY. WILL BE HOME ALL TOO SOON M & D

Your story may be used during the performance.

Thank you

Jodie & Pete
Search Party

If you would like to contribute to *Save Me* please answer these questions, put the form back in the plastic wallet. Our stewards will lend you a pen if...

Who are you apart from?

MYSELF

Where are they now?

lost

What would you like to say to...

Act

Your story may be used during the...

Thank you

Jodie & Pete
Search Party

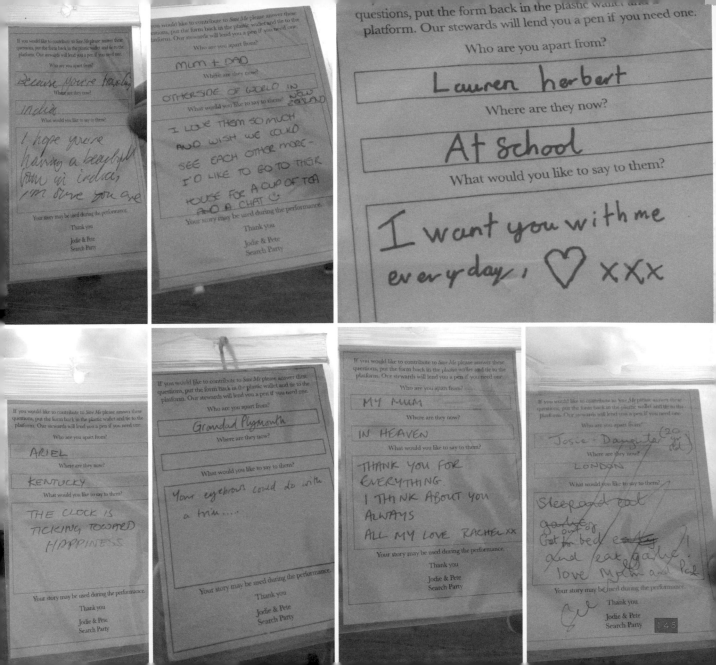

Jesus in
—heaven

Please
come
back
soon!

If you would like to contribute to *Save Me* please answer these questions, put the form back in the plastic wallet and tie to the platform. Our stewards will lend you a pen if you need one.

Who are you apart from?
Family

Where are they now?
Brunei

What would you like to say to them?
Mom and dad,
We missed you both so much! Pray that we'll be home soon. Please wait for us!
Love,
Monica & Peter

Your story may be used during the performance.

Thank you
Jodie & Pete
Search Party

If you would like to contribute to *Save Me* please answer these questions, put the form back in the plastic wallet and tie to the platform. Our stewards will lend you a pen if you need one.

Who are you apart from?
MY AUNT

Where are they now?
IN A HOME

What would you like to say to them?
I MISS YOU, BE PATIENT, REMEMBER THE GOOD TIMES & EMBRACE THE COMPANY

Your story may be used during the performance.

Thank you
Jodie & Pete
Search Party

If you would like to contribute to *Save Me* please answer these questions, put the form back in the plastic wallet and tie to the platform. Our stewards will lend you a pen if you need one.

Who are you apart from?
My Great Aunty

Where are they now?
In heaven.

What would you like to say to them?
Thankyou.

Your story may be used during the performance.

Thank you
Jodie & Pete
Search Party

If you would like to contribute to *Save Me* please answer these questions, put the form back in the plastic wallet and tie to the platform. Our stewards will lend you a pen if you need one.

Who are you apart from?
MY BEST FRIEND

Where are they now?
IN ANOTHER CITY

What would you like to say to them?
I CAN'T WAIT TO MEET THE NEW PERSON TINY FINGERS + TOES I'VE RIGHT BESIDE YA ALWAYS AND LOOKING ON IN AWE.

Your story may be used during the performance.

Thank you
Jodie & Pete
Search Party

If you would like to contribute to *Save Me* please answer these questions, put the form back in the plastic wallet and tie to the platform. Our stewards will lend you a pen if you need one.

Who are you apart from?
I'm tempted to say No one

Where are they now?
Nowhere + Everywhere

What would you like to say to them?
I'm working on my sense of connectedness, Do not worry.

Your story may be used during the performance.

Thank you
Jodie & Pete
Search Party

If you would like to contribute to *Save Me* please answer these questions, put the form back in the plastic wallet and tie to the platform. Our stewards will lend you a pen if you need one.

Who are you apart from?
Dad

Where are they now?
Living in Spain

What would you like to say to them?
I miss having you near and being able to see you.

Your story may be used during the performance.

Thank you
Jodie & Pete
Search Party

If you would like to contribute to *Save Me* please answer these questions, put the form back in the plastic wallet and tie to the platform. Our stewards will lend you a pen if you need one.

Who are you apart from?

MY BROTHER

Where are they now?

What would you like to say to them?

ICH VERMISSE DICH

Your story may be used during the performance

Thank you
Jodie & Pete
Search Party

If you would like to contribute to *Save Me* please answer these questions, put the form back in the plastic wallet and tie to the platform. Our stewards will lend you a pen if you need one.

Who are you apart from?

Jim Scull

Where are they now?

At home! ♡

What would you like to say to them?

Thankyou again for helping me through all the tough times. I sure hope I can do the same for you. ♡ I love you! xx

Your story may be used during the performance

Thank you
Jodie & Pete
Search Party

If you would like to contribute to *Save Me* please answer these questions, put the form back in the plastic wallet and tie to the platform. Our stewards will lend you a pen if you need one.

Who are you apart from?

Lynne

Where are they now?

driving back from Yorkshire

What would you like to say to them?

Im glad your dads cancer is treatable. I hope your journey is safe. I love you madly, deeply, truly. Laszlo xx

Your story may be used during the performance

Thank you
Jodie & Pete
Search Party

If you would like to contribute to *Save Me* please answer these questions, put the form back in the plastic wallet and tie to the platform. Our stewards will lend you a pen if you need one.

Who are you apart from?

BEHLA

Where are they now?

LEEDS

What would you like to say to them?

I LOVE YOU + I'VE NEVER STOPPED LOVING YOU. GET SOME FUCKS!

Your story may be used during the performance

Thank you
Jodie & Pete
Search Party

If you would like to contribute to *Save Me* please answer these questions, put the form back in the plastic wallet and tie to the platform. Our stewards will lend you a pen if you need one.

Who are you apart from?

my parents

Where are they now?

andre + hunderous Singapore

What would you like to say to them?

we miss each other but the good thing is that now we are learning to communicate that, + that we love each other. xoxo

Your story may be used during the performance

Thank you
Jodie & Pete
Search Party

If you would like to contribute to *Save Me* please answer these questions, put the form back in the plastic wallet and tie to the platform. Our stewards will lend you a pen if you need one.

Who are you apart from?

My friend Anna

Where are they now?

Kenya

What would you like to say to them?

Don't worry about me

147

If you would like to contribute to *Save Me* please answer these questions, put the form back in the plastic wallet and tie to the platform. Our stewards will lend you a pen if you need one.

Who are you apart from?

MONIQE

Where are they now?

WITH PETE

What would you like to say to them?

FEET SORE. CATCHING NEXT BOAT TO NOVA SCOTIA. HIDE THE DATA ELIMINATE THE CONTACT. SEE YOU ON THE FLIP

Your story may be used during the performance.

Thank you

Jodie & Pete
Search Party

If you would like to contribute to *Save Me* please answer these questions, put the form back in the plastic wallet and tie to the platform. Our stewards will lend you a pen if you need one.

Who are you apart from?

Macbeth

Where are they now?

half way across the world!

What would you like to say to them?

Bring forth men children only & I wish things were different!

Your story may be used during the performance.

Thank you

Jodie & Pete
Search Party

If you would like to contribute to *Save Me* please answer these questions, put the form back in the plastic wallet and tie to the platform. Our stewards will lend you a pen if you need one.

Who are you apart from?

A LOVELY MAN

Where are they now?

TOO NEAR BUT TOO FAR

What would you like to say to them?

CAN WE BE TOGETHER IN ANOTHER LIFE?

Your story may be used during the performance.

Thank you

Jodie & Pete
Search Party

If you would like to contribute to *Save Me* please answer these questions, put the form back in the plastic wallet and tie to the platform. Our stewards will lend you a pen if you need one.

Who are you apart from?

Lexi chambers.

Where are they now?

London.

What would you like to say to them?

I want to talk to you again. The Knight Rider REALLY misses you! Love Tim.

Your story may be used during the performance.

 Thank you

Jodie & Pete
Search Party

MY NEIGHBOUR SOPHIE

Where are they now?

THE STREET I USED TO LIVE ON

What would you like to say to them?

THANKYOU FOR COMING OUT WHEN YOU HEARD ME CALLING FOR HELP, THANKYOU FOR TAKING ME IN AND MOPPING MY BLOOD, THANKYOU FOR CALLING 999 YOU HELPED TO SAVE MY LIFE.

Your story may be used during the performance.

Thank you

Who are you apart from?

Daniel

Where are they now?

chi

What would you like to say to them?

Stop being such an alcholic.

Your story may be used during the performance.

Thank you

Jodie & Pete
Search Party

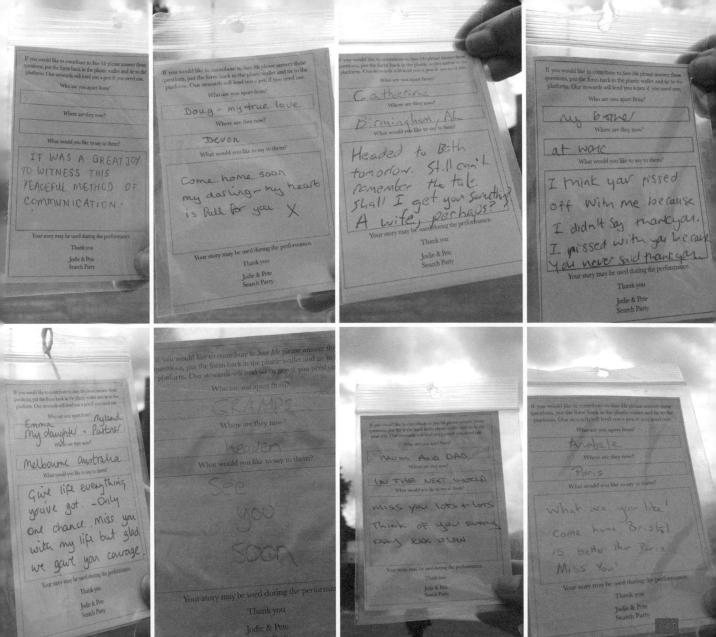

SECTION 4:
AFTERWORD

Three months after those 11, long, arm aching days in May, we travelled to Tasmania to play table tennis (*Search Party vs Launceston*).

Before this our feet had never left the Northern Hemisphere. All the time with the nagging thought in our minds that we would have to think of something to write here on this page, to introduce you the reader to our practice…

Well it was wonderful in Tasmania. There's something to be said for travelling all the way to the other side of the world just to see clearly what it is that you are doing all the way back home. Something about all that space and clean air in Tassie, encouraged us to find some space in our heads, to consider and re-consider *Save Me* and how the work fits more broadly into our practice. And maybe there's something to be said for reflecting on a practice that's interested simultaneously in duration and ephemerality on an epic 23-hour long-haul flight with turbulence so bad that the thought that we might drop out of the sky at any moment is a constant worry. We've discovered that describing a practice from the inside is harder than it might seem. So we've enlisted the help of a couple of people who know us well to write alongside us, to draw out reoccurring themes, to share memories and to make playful insights into Search Party's work.
Pete & Jodie (Search Party)

1> The basics
(*a description)
Search Party are a flag waving, ping pong playing, salt rubbing, whale watching, bus loving, moon orbiting, rhino running family whose interest lies somewhere between wanting things to last forever (or at least as long as the performance) and wanting to sneak off for a cuppa whilst no-one's looking. They are based in Bristol, where they go to book clubs, practice their table tennis (think you can beat Jodie? Wrong.) and take their daughter to see the ducks.
Gemma Paintin (Action Hero)

2> Sore eyes
(*intimacy and distance)
As we look back over the performance projects that have characterised the first six years of our collaboration, it seems that we've always been interested in intimacy and distance. In our first work I was the moon and you were the command module and joined together by string tied around our waists, you orbited me (*The Long Walk to the Performance*). Or in sharing a private moment through a single spy hole along the length of a 12m x 0.5m home-made corridor (*Corridor*). Or when, like Olympic track cyclists, we chased each other around Lavender Hill on buses, a loving pursuit around a mile-long circuit (*Outside*). Or more recently, in the recording of closing speeches to end a life-long project that has only just begun (*Growing Old With You*). And then creating something both intimate and epic across the length of St Augustine's Reach, Bristol – using flagged symbols to discuss our enforced separation (*Save Me*). And I'm not sure what we've learnt about intimacy and distance, in fact it seems that the closer we are the less we talk. But in these repeated attempts to describe our own experience of intimacy, and the simultaneous attempt to stretch them out across physical and temporal distances we reveal ourselves, we are vulnerable and in these spaces we are

'Search Party vs Newcastle'

'Growing old with you'

'The Long Walk to the Performance'

LUNA

'Keep Going the Rhino!'

'Search Party vs Newcastle'

153

able to communicate something that feels important with an audience.
Pete Phillips (Search Party)

3> Arm Ache
(*effort and labour)
The arm is an amazingly adaptable tool. But after 11 days of flag waving I have muscle fatigue. But then again there has always been an interest in the sort of effort, the sort of labour, the sort of duration that necessitates a long post-performance soak in a nice warm bath. In the endless tirade of tragic stories about a made-up man called Trevor, the repeated soaking with half full/half empty cups of water until we are beyond wet through and the relentless attempts to light candles on a birthday cake with wet fingers and wetter matches (*The Long Walk to the Performance*). In the laps of a track I run until my feet blister, all the time you're shouting 'KEEP GOING JODIE'S HEART, JODIE'S LUNGS, JODIE'S FEET' (*Keep Going The Rhino!*). In the endless laps of Lavender Hill, a performance that doesn't stop until we catch one another (*Outside*), and the repeated back and forth, back and forth along a home-made corridor (*Corridor*). Or in the marathon 3-day Ping-Pong matches where I play for so long and you speak for so long that I start to feel time slowing down and the ball becomes the size of a beach ball and you need to drink Lemsip in

between the hoarse, raspy warm up texts (*Search Party vs …*). And then in the salt that stings your eyes, dulls your taste buds and can be found days later in ear holes and between toes, never quite washed away (*Growing Old With You*). As if all this effort, all this labour is making the performance matter somehow. Or an acknowledgment that in this effort there is frailty, failure, accidents, mistakes, an inability to move the arm you want, forgetfulness, unrecognizability of a letter, of a word — moments where despite, of and perhaps because of, the effort and the labour the thing starts to break down — but at least we're trying.
Jodie Hawkes (Search Party)

4> 11 Long Days
(*duration and place)
The drinkers in the bars, the cyclists, the tourists, the walkers, the strollers, the parents with their pushchairs and their children all glance across the water, drawn to the unusual sight of a man in red waving semaphore flags. But over the course of 11 days something changes. Like our 3-day marathon public Ping-Pong tournaments (*Search Party vs…*), my flag waving on Pero's bridge, at first an oddity becomes familiar. It's a simple thing we're doing — talking with flags. But we're here day after day, same time, same place. And perhaps it is in the repeated dipping in and out of the

project that makes it seem like something bigger – a part of the furniture. A convincing illusion because when so suddenly we are gone there is a gap, something has changed – like when the trees lining St Augustine's Reach have been too severely pollarded, providing more light and less shade, this place feels different. Or when thousands of amateur runners are plodding round St Augustine's parade, inspired or irritated by Heart FM's cheery pop classics, this place feels different. Like the pruned trees and the sweaty runners, us flag wavers reshape this place, in a way that is perhaps best measured by the moment of our absence.
Pete Phillips (Search Party)

5> The People of this Place
(*audience and place)
Across a table tennis table in the Market Square in the centre of Kuopio, Finland we meet a 17-year old trainee plumber called Matti (*Search Party vs Kuopio*). Matti, who having taken up our challenge and won a game of table tennis against us, called all his friends and told them to come down. Minutes later we hear the hum of teenagers on mopeds – the cavalry had arrived. Over the next three days he returns, he brings different people with him – as if when our backs are turned he's whizzing around on his

moped, scouring the city for decent players to represent Kuopio. It seems to matter to him. And each time we heard the sound of mopeds echo across the square we knew Matti, the hometown hero, was on his way back. To the point where he is as recognisable as us, and when people return to have another go or check on the score, they are relived that Matti is still here. And of course its not just Matti, every city or town we challenge has it's own heroes, people who become household names in the enduring narrative of these 3-day table tennis performances.
Pete Phillips (Search Party)

6> The SEE SAW
(*process: rehearsing whilst potty training)
Since having a third (very lively) person between us (our daughter) we've had to re-negotiate our working process. We've had to find other ways and spaces to communicate with one another. Conversations no longer take place in the rehearsal room (yet I'm not sure they ever did), now it's in the park across either end of the sea saw or long walks pushing a pram. And now with a (walking, talking) toddler we're finding that again there's need for new re-negotiations on how we might communicate. For a while we've been making work through a series of letters to each other, simple

conversations stretched out of whole days or weeks despite our physical proximity. Understanding and misunderstanding each other, all the time, moving between closeness and distance, snatching pockets of time to work, to talk, to be together. And realising all the time that we are one of thousands, millions of people who are separated from loved ones, in whatever way you might take that to mean. And so the lines between work and life are increasingly blurred and it's impossible to talk about one without the other.
Jodie Hawkes (Search Party)

7> The Free Lunch
(*the performance duo and their dramaturg)
"So the deal is you work with us…. NO, not all the time." Pete's face flickers (very slightly) with panic for a second. "… but on a number of days throughout the year. You drive to Bristol, sit in a basement, read fragments from my note book or from Jodie's note book; you see things 'on-their-feet' and … well … you dramaturg." "Is 'dramaturg' a verb?" I ask. "I don't know, but that's the kind of question you could usefully raise as part of the dramaturgical process." "Oh… right." Silence. "Then you drive home". "When?" "After you've finishing dramaturging." "If dramaturg is a verb." Silence. "So, does a

dramaturg get paid?" Longer silence. "Well, we could put it into the next grant application: how much do you charge?" "I don't know." "Oh." Interminable Silence. Jodie joins in: "We'll pay your petrol." Pause. "And…" Awkward pause that borders on silence "…we'll buy you lunch." I brighten: "What… every time I come?" Awkward pause, bordering on silence, combined with a shared look between Pete and Jodie (a look that I get to know very well over the next eighteen months). "Yes" says Pete, with a hint of wait-till-I-get-you-home menace. "EVERY time…" "So, there is such a thing as a FREE LUNCH: ha ha ha ha …." Stop laughing. Silence.

19 March 2010: St Nicholas Market. Pie Minister. Ben has the last Steak and Ale Pie, Pete and Ben (No Jodie). Awkward. Will Pete get his wallet out? He does. Working on Growing Old with You. Letters to each other. One-on-one performance from Pete (43 Candles: the Victoria sponge sets on fire). We arrive at the idea of preservation. Salt? 'Can we hang you, Pete?' 'Er…okay.'

7 July 2010: St Nicholas Market. Pie Minister (but Jodie wants a rather boring sandwich from elsewhere, which she doesn't eat). Pete wears the same shirt. Jokes about the University

of Chichester buying him a shirt (or a MacBook). Working on *Growing Old*. On the roof of the Old Vic. Not quite getting to work… Recapping what's happened at Mayfest. 'Did you get to hang, Pete?' 'No.' Building towards Forest Fringe. 'Can we hang you at Forest Fringe, Pete?' Collective decision that it might not be best to try hanging Pete at the health-and-safety-free-zone of Forest Fringe. Write Text. Quite good actually…

21 August 2010: Edinburgh. Sandwiches from Tesco Express (missing Pie Minister…. Missing Bristol, frankly). Out on the Meadows: rehearsing *Growing Old* – feels strange to be 'rehearsing', but that's what we're doing. Student-theatre groups watching, think it's a performance. They don't get it. We do. Pete and Jodie talk quietly to themselves. Feel like a director. They feel like actors.

27 November 2010: St Nicholas Market. All bored with Pie Minister But we still go to Pie Minister. Building to Inbetween Time. Text (again). We cut the idea of hanging Pete. Pity. Smoke. Some talk of working on *Save Me*. It needs a text. Or does it?

11 March 2011: St Nicholas Market. Moroccan takeaway. Feeling liberated. *Save Me*. Keywords: Bristol; Semaphore; Nautical; Harbour (or Suspension Bridge?); separation; living

apart; including people, but how? Different from London, but how? 10 Days (or is it 11?). Feeling liberated at the end of the day.

13 April 2011: My Burrito, Broad Quay. Stepping out of our St Nicholas comfort-zone. A field-trip/site-visit. Feels along way from home. Very public. Feeling people are watching us, even now. Matthew and Kate take us to another level. A man wants to talk about semaphore, based on seeing the rolled-up flags. Might as well have been in Mexico.

19 April 2011: Back in St Nicholas Market, but we can't go back to pies now: something Spanish. In the basement at the Old Vic. Flags, flags, flags. Timings. Logistics. In the corner, writing, keeping out the way. We're ready. We're not ready. I'm keeping out the way.

15 June 2011: On my own. The funding has dried up. Pete and Jodie bring lasagne from home. There's only enough for two. I go back to Pie Minister. Arnolfini are interested in the book, so are we. Reading the tags. Don't get much further. Too many ideas. Almost worth paying for my own lunch.

Ben Francombe (Dramaturg, Search Party)

8> Walking through Easton
(*remnants and remains)

Two days after I turn 30, and one day after I have a party to celebrate, I'm walking through Easton in Bristol, hungover, with a friend. We've been to a barbecue. It's a hot July day. Easton is inner-city Bristol, a mile or so from the harbourside. It's often described as a melting pot. As we stroll along the street, making silly jokes and chatting about nothing in particular, I notice something very familiar. Wedged behind the road sign for St Mark's Terrace, on a small side road miles from where it had been created, is half of one of the *Save Me* boards from Sunday 15th May, the final day of the performance. Slightly weather-beaten, a bit scuffed, and roughly chopped in half, Pete's words still stand out in bright yellow.

I wonder how it got there, how long Pete and Jodie's words had been welcoming people into St Mark's Terrace, and whether anyone else had stopped for a moment and tried to figure out what it all meant. I'm suddenly really moved by seeing it. Perhaps it's my fragile hungover emotions, but in that moment, it all comes flooding back - seeing that board, that fragment of conversation far away from where it was created, half-way between being trash and street art - the simplicity and the beauty of those messages passing

across the water, and the strange comfort I had taken in seeing Pete and Jodie on the bridge and the harbourside every morning as I dashed around Bristol in the chaos of the festival. In works like *Search Party Vs…*, *Growing Old With You*, as well as *Save Me*, Search Party seem to be increasingly interested in the residue of these ephemeral acts, in what is left behind, in how these people and these places are changed.
Matthew Austin (Mayfest)

'Search Party vs Kuopio'

CREDITS

Save Me:
A Conversation Across the City
A Search Party Project

Compiled by
Pete Phillips, Jodie Hawkes and Ben
Francombe

Designed by
Graham Roy Donaldson

Individual Written Contributions
Kate Yedigaroff
Holly Ponder
Pete Phillips
Gemma Paintin
Saini Manninen
Jodie Hawkes
Ben Francombe
Jennie Dick
Matthew Austin

Photography and Other Images
James Stenhouse
Rules & Regs
Thom Pearson
Gemma Paintin
Pekka Makinen
Rachael Lynch
Toby Farrow
Rob Edwards
Graham Roy Donaldson
Donna Kirstein
Nic Burke
Jim Banks
Paul Avery
Kerrie Avery
Claudio Ahlers

Book produced by
Search Party and the
University of Chichester

Printed in UK by
MWL Print Group Units 10-13
Pontyfelin Industrial Estate New Inn
Pontypool NP4 0DQ
Tel: 01495 750033
Fax: 01495 751466
www.mwl.co.uk

Published by Arnolfini
16 Narrow Quay
Bristol BS1 4QA, UK
Tel +44 (0)117 917 2300
Fax +44 (0)117 917 2303
www.arnolfini.org.uk

Distributed by
Cornerhouse Publications
70 Oxford Road
Manchester M1 5NH, UK
Tel +44 (0)161 200 1503
Fax +44 (0)161 200 1504
www.cornerhouse.org

Save Me (Mayfest 2011)
commissioned by Mayfest and
Theatre Bristol

Development Support by
Home Live Art and Rules and Regs

**Thank you to the following
individuals**
Kate Yedigaroff, Dion Wilson,
Sarah Warden, Claire Teasdale,
Chris Swain, James Stenhouse,
Mel Scaffold, Thom Pearson,
Gemma Paintin, Georgina Monro,
Charlotte McShane, Holly McGrane,
Mike Martins, Anna Lambert,
Donna Kirstei, Katie Keeler,
Abigail Hill, Ruth Hennell, Nikki Grant,
Jennie Dick, Kerrie Avery,
Matthew Austin, Helen Aspell,
Tim X Atack and Tanuja Amarasuriya.

BIOGRAPHIES

Search Party

Search Party is the collaboration of artists Pete Phillips and Jodie Hawkes. Since 2005 Search Party have created performances for studio, gallery and public space throughout the UK, Europe and Australia. Search Party are committed to making immediate, hopeful performances that engage broad and diverse audiences. We often return to ideas of place, duration and intimacy. We are members of Residence, an artist-led organisation based in Bristol, comprising of artists and companies who make theatre, performance and live art.
www.searchpartyperformance.org.uk
www.residence.org.uk

Ben Francombe

Ben Francombe is Principal Lecturer and Head of Performing Arts at the University of Chichester. Previously he worked at Bretton Hall in West Yorkshire, where he first met Pete Phillips and Jodie Hawkes and made them do things in the name of education he now regrets. He has twenty-years experience of dramaturgy and artist support and continues, through his work with the Showroom (University of Chichester), to work with a range of artists, most recently the Paper Birds and 1927. He has worked as dramaturg for two Search Party projects: *Save Me* and *Growing Old with You*.

Graham Roy Donaldson (Design)

Graham Roy Donaldson is a graphic designer with more than sixteen-years experience, working both in Britain (London) and Australia (Sydney). He loves life and graphic design. He has loved working with Search Party on this project.

The University of Chichester, Department of Performing Arts (Co-Producer)

The Department of Performing Arts runs the highly successful BA Performing Arts (Theatre Performance) and MA Performance (Theatre and Theatre Collectives); it also offers supervision in MPhil/PhD, primarily in Contemporary Performance Practice as Research. The Department runs the Showroom, a national touring venue and artist-support centre. The Showroom has offered extensive support to a large number of performing artists, including Action Hero, Search Party, the Paper Birds, 1927, Bootworks, Beady Eye, Stacy Makishi, Milk, Punchdrunk, Spy Monkey, Tinned Fingers, Wide Eyes Collective, Lila Dance, Reckless Sleepers, Bill Aitchison, Gregory Maqoma and Sidi Larbi.
www.chi.ac.uk/performingarts
www.theshowroomchichester.co.uk

Arnolfini - A Space For Ideas

Since its foundation in 1961, Arnolfini has built an international reputation for commissioning and presenting innovative, risk-taking work. Its mission is 'to foster artistic experiment and engagement across the contemporary arts'. Through a multidisciplinary programme of exhibitions, live art, dance, music, film, poetry and literature, with a strong emphasis upon learning and participation, Arnolfini provides Bristol and the West of England with a centre for the contemporary arts of international significance. Arnolfini is dedicated to championing new art and new ideas, and to making artistic excellence and innovation accessible for all.
www.arnolfini.org.uk

Mayfest

Mayfest is an annual festival of contemporary performance which takes place in Bristol, UK. It commissions and presents a broad range of unusual, playful and ambitious work from leading theatre makers from Bristol, the UK and beyond. Mayfest is produced by MAYK in collaboration with Bristol Old Vic and works in partnership with venues across Bristol to present work in established theatre and non-theatre spaces all over the city.

In autumn 2010, Mayfest and Theatre Bristol got together to discuss the possibility of collaborating on commissioning a new performance for Mayfest 2011. We decided that we wanted to work with a South West artist or company to develop an outdoor project; a project which re-imagines what outdoor theatre could be; something which engages with the city in which it is performed; and something which we could support in its future life. It was a tough selection procedure - we received some excellent proposals - but one stood out, a seemingly small, simple idea by Search Party for a durational semaphore soap opera which would run through the festival. The realisation of Save Me exceeded all our expectations - an outdoor work which managed to be both epic and intimate, celebratory and almost unbearably moving. We couldn't have asked for a better project to mark our first collaboration as commissioners. www.mayfestbristol.co.uk

Theatre Bristol

Theatre Bristol is an independent organisation which commissions and produces new work across the spectrum of performance (from circus to soundwalks), offers bespoke artist support and training, runs a dynamic user-generated web resource, undertakes strategic research, and develops national and international exchange opportunities. www.theatrebristol.net

Home Live Art

From our roots in the domestic context to work with festivals, galleries, theatres and public spaces, home live art produces work in diverse contexts and environments, playfully referencing traditional, communal and celebratory forms that question and challenge whilst remaining wholly accessible to all.

In a new partnership with The Mayor's Thames Festival, home live art commissioned three new pieces of work by artists: Amy Sharrocks, Search Party and Tim Etchells.

Using the River Thames as a point of reference, a resource and a location, each artist created a temporary work exploring our relationship to water. A River Enquiry was a key feature of the Mayor's Thames Festival, London's largest free outdoor arts festival. www.homeliveart.com

Rules and Regs

Rules and Regs creates innovative programmes supporting artists' development. R&R brings artists, organisations and audiences together, fostering understanding and creativity through making and experiencing new art, in new ways. R&R's primary programme - from which the company takes its name - is Rules and Regs: a residency in which participating artists make new work in response to rules devised by a curator as a challenge to explore new ways of working. Each month-long programme is curated by a different organisation and culminates in a public exhibition of work. www.rulesandregs.org/shp11.html

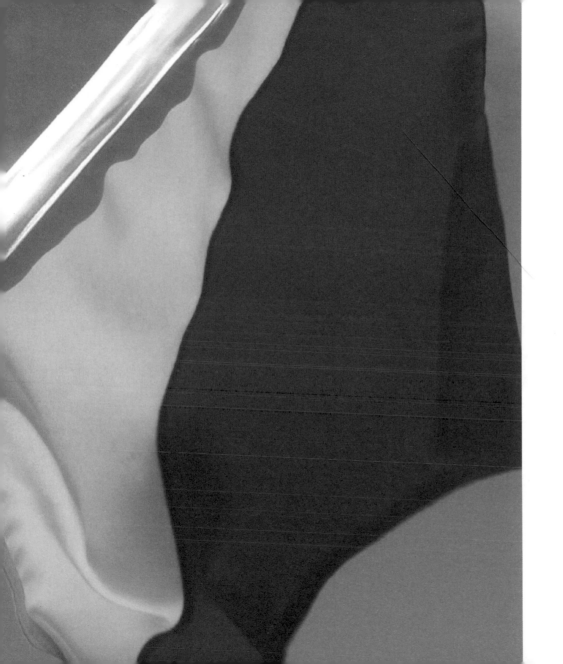

ARNOLFINI 50

University of Chichester

Mayfest

THEATRE
BRISTOL

home

* Rules and Regs

residence